Danielle Collins

C000050660

How to
REALLY
Go With The
FLOW

A Philosophy for Living a Magically Authentic Life.

How to REALLY Go With The Flow

The book information is catalogued as follows;

Author Name(s): Danielle Collins

How to REALLY Go With The Flow

Description; First Edition

1st Edition, 2021

Book Design by Lynda Mangoro

Cover Art by Danielle Collins

ISBN: 978-1-914447-17-4

ISBN (ebook): 978-1-914447-18-1

Published by That Guy's House

www.ThatGuysHouse.com

How to
REALLY
Go With The
FLOW

This one's for my Sue's!

Thank you for always believing in me, just like Gump did. For supporting me through all my mad ideas and sudden changes. For sending Team Sparkle to the rescue! For having a laugh with me at the many ridiculous situations we got ourselves into along the way. For being the best Mummy, who 'loves me kids' no matter what.

I bloody loves you xx

Contents

Prologue: Fuck Being Perfect

"Peach, nobody likes a 'perfect' person."

This could be one of the best pieces of advice my Dad has ever given me. Because it is so true! 'Perfect' people make me suspicious. It just doesn't add up. Where's their dark side? What are they hiding? It just feels false.

Some people even try to polish up their 'bad bits' and make that seem 'perfect' and then sell the 'how to guide' to others – 'this is how you can be perfect like me'. Creating yet more fake clones.

So called 'spiritual gurus' have a lot to answer for if you ask me. We are ALL both student AND teacher in every interaction. No-one is ever completely 'enlightened' and has all the answers because their soul wouldn't need to be here anymore. It's dangerous and misleading to think otherwise. I'm SICK of all the lies!

But the compassionate part of me knows that they are struggling to be authentic too. They may believe that their success depends on them, 'holding their shit together'. Maybe they do actually have their shit together? I doubt that very much.

Because behind the scenes, let's face it- we're all crumbling messes of wild emotions trying to make it look like we are adults who can cope well with life. But the truth is NOT coping with life, IS coping with life. Showing and sharing your emotions is part of being human and this needs to be normalised and celebrated.

It is people's flaws that draw us in, the quirks, the weird shit, the fuck ups. That is, if they REALLY own it. We all know that the thing that makes that person not 'perfect' is the thing we LOVE the most about them. And yet, for some strange reason we all try and hide our flaws like they are shameful secrets never to be seen. This makes me really sad, and a little angry.

Why is it that the world is so fucked up that being your most authentic self is actually one of, if not, the hardest things to do?

I've battled with this myself. BIG time. I still do if I am totally honest, I notice myself holding back when I should speak up. Or trying to present myself in a certain way to be liked. Despite a whole lot of therapy, healing, study and many a meltdown to get to the point where I refuse to live a lie anymore, it is STILL a daily challenge. But I am determined to master this. To master being me.

Because living a lie (toned down or fake version of myself) may please others but the price is too big. It hurts me, it hurts my soul, my inner child and I'm not prepared to do that anymore. I've made some good progress, but I am under no illusion that there is still more work to be done.

Because being truly authentic is not something you can achieve overnight unfortunately, it's a gradual process of many small changes made over time. Step by step peeling back the layers. But I've made a firm commitment to myself to move towards embracing my authentic self more and more each day, no matter what the consequences.

Oh, and there are consequences! Being your most authentic unique self, triggers the fuck out of the people around you. This is why you are here! To push people's buttons, to get them to wake-up, to provoke a reaction, to shake-up the status quo, to be a catalyst for change and healing for others.

Now don't get me wrong, I don't go around intentionally upsetting people and hurting their feelings. I try my best to be authentic in a kind and sensitive way (and I have admittedly failed to do this on many occasions, for which I am sorry and have learned from, I'm not perfect) but no matter how you deliver your truth, it is often the case that it will provoke some kind of reaction in others. Often a defensive stance or anger. You've hit a sore spot. That's OK, don't let people's reactions stop you from speaking and sharing your truth. Some people will run for the hills, others will really appreciate you for it. Some may run and then come back later to thank you.

At first, you will have many a bad experience of truth-telling, you're in training, mistakes are how you learn. When you are a little more seasoned in this way of being, you ooze such a powerful, self-assured presence that people no longer question you in the same way. When you deliver the truth in a respectful calm manner people can't help but listen and admire you for it. But it takes practice and a lot of fuck ups to learn how to do it well. And even then, every situation is different so there is always more to learn.

Even when you are getting good at it, some people still stubbornly refuse to accept the offer of having true, authentic relationships in their life, preferring to 'play the fake game'. To keep trying to fit in and 'do the right thing' to be seen as more acceptable to society. To avoid facing their demons. I'm not even sure they realise they are doing it or that they have a choice in the matter. But you can't fight other people's battles for them. Been there, tried that, still have to stop myself from doing it ALL the time.

Sadly, most people, in my experience, do not want to take the many risks involved with joining the 'honest club'. Being properly honest means you will lose a few people along the way. People who aren't ready to take the leap of faith that is required to live this way. To risk losing something that isn't actually right for them anyway, in the quest for something that is. Most people prefer to play it safe and cling to what they have, instead of jumping into the unknown and trusting that something better is on its way. Even when that something doesn't immediately present itself.

FYI...The new thing won't appear until you are ready. The key here is to stay with the uncomfortable emotions that arise from the fear of the unknown and keep trusting.

I've put this theory to the test soooooo many times now I have total faith and trust in the process. It is a never-ending cycle of letting go of the old and surrendering to the new. I'm calling it, 'REALLY going with the flow'.

Now, just because I have been through this cycle a million times does not mean that it necessarily gets any easier. In some ways it does, because I know what to do now to make the journey a little smoother, but there is always discomfort in growth. Every cycle cracks you open a little bit more, it tests you to face your deepest, darkest fears and emotions. Which, by the way, isn't half as bad as avoiding them!

So back to my point on being perfect – nobody likes a perfect person because we all know- that shit just isn't real. No matter how polished and shiny we make ourselves look, we are energetic beings who know when something is off. It doesn't feel good for you or the people you are interacting with.

And you can't build real intimacy, connection and relationships based on bullshit.

Showing your vulnerability is the way to truly connect with others. This requires a lot of courage, tissues and difficult conversations. Because we are all floundering in some way, shape or form. Life is challenging and the more honest we can be about that with each other, the more we can help one another.

I am on a mission to lead by example. To just be me. To be real. To speak my truth, my whole truth and nothing but the truth, no matter what. And to learn to love and forgive myself for the times when I can't quite manage it yet. A part of me still wants to please and be liked, especially with new people I find. Also, some people are easier to be honest around, and with, than others. So many things affect your ability to speak your truth in any given situation. We can only do our best, as the flawed human beings that we are.

Which leads me nicely on to the book cover – far from perfect, trust me, I know! I'm feeling super shy and awkward to share it. But I also love it. It feels like me. My energy, my childlike excitement for life, my risk- taking self. And there's a 'going with the flow' story behind how this cover came to be (of course!).

Originally, I had an idea in mind for the book cover and asked a close friend, who also happens to be an amazing graphic designer, to bring it to life for me. She spent many loving hours translating my ideas into a design she thought I would love. I hoped I would love it too but had a feeling I wouldn't. When she sent it through, I was disappointed. It wasn't it at all. It was her energy behind it and not mine. How could anyone create my energy but me? I tried sending her some more images of things I liked, but deep down I knew it wasn't ever going to feel right.

In an attempt to shed some light on this situation, I sat down with my box of creative bits and bobs. Mostly pens, crayons, and other random things found in the kids' section of craft shops I had collected over the summer. I sat in bed and asked the question – what does 'going with the flow' look like? Then I just got to work, choosing whatever colour I wanted and letting loose. I wasn't creating with the intention of sharing it. This was just for fun and for me to understand flow in a visual way. It didn't take me long, I just allowed myself to play until it felt complete. I liked it but I didn't think I would actually ever use it for anything. I put it away for a while and continued to contemplate what to do about the cover.

Until it dawned on me, that WAS the front cover. I was not impressed by this idea at first. I thought, 'Oh no, no way!' I cannot share this random scribble with the world. I was embarrassed and apologetic of my creativity. But I could not deny that every time I looked at it, it made me smile. If nothing else, my book cover may just make people smile. Is that such a bad thing? Nothing else felt right and this did. It was going to take a big dose of courage and a massive leap of faith to run with this but luckily, I am a naturally optimistic risk-taker, so I thought fuck it. If we are going to be authentic, might as well go the whole hog! Is that a saying?! Yes, apparently it means to do something thoroughly and without restraint. Ha, I love it. That, in my opinion, is how life should be lived.

A Little Heads-Up

The first 30 years of my life were spent learning how it felt to go against the flow. To have strong instinctual responses but to ignore them. This wasn't a conscious thing.

I would often talk to people who were saying one thing, while I was feeling something very different from them energetically. I assumed my feelings were wrong and their words were right.

This landed me in many a bad friendship, relationship, job, you name it.

Until I realised that ALL those times I had doubted myself were actually my incredibly valuable training ground to learn how to trust myself. To honour my feelings, and my truth, above and beyond what anyone or anything else was trying to convince me of.

So here is what I have learnt about 'really going with the flow'.

How to Use This Book

Flow comes in four parts.

Part 1: Let's Get Flowing

Here you get to meet Flow and learn about each of the 4 stages of her Philosophy, explained through the use of Tarot, Astrology, the Elements, the Seasons, channelled messages and real-life stories.

Part 2: Let's Get Realistic

My own personal story of how I found Flow and what flowing through each stage can actually look like in reality. Brace yourselves!

Part 3: Let's Get Connected

To really flow, you need to have a strong connection to your own intuition and your creativity. This section offers useful insights and exercises for you to explore.

Part 4: Let's Get Practical

The spiritual survival kit and skills you will need to learn and to master to make Flow life a bit more bearable! This includes self-healing techniques, divination tools and more.

Now, just because you can read Flow in one sitting doesn't mean you should. Take your time with her, feel her out. Trust when enough is enough and save the rest for another day.

Flow is all about divine timing, so this book has found you at the perfect time, but please be mindful that there is no rush to digest all that she has to offer.

Once read, she can be a wonderful travel companion for you through your flow journey. Pick her up and open her at random when you are in need of some support or cheering up. Or just to remind yourself of the basics.

She's yours to enjoy now. Make yourself super comfy, maximise the pleasure of reading her with a nice drink, a notebook and pen by your side, soft lighting, whatever makes you feel good. When she's not in use, continue to absorb her magically healing energy by displaying her somewhere that makes you smile.

Above all else, have fun with her! Now, let's flow.

PART 1

Let's Get Flowing

Introducing my Mate, Flow

Going with the flow is how life is meant to be lived, in my opinion. It's our most natural state of being.

Returning to our true intuitive nature.

But let me start by saying 'going with the flow' is not the blissful boat trip down a beautifully calm river that the saying implies. Oh no.

Far from it actually.

It's much more like a crazy bumpy ride on the dodgems where you are speeding along one minute and then crash and bang into obstacles constantly, get stuck in a jam, then have to back-up and try a new direction again and again. You may feel bruised and battered along the way.

That is the reality of going with the flow. It definitely *isn't* as easy as it sounds.

But if you ask me, the rewards outweigh all of the challenges.

The biggest reward being, that you get to be the real, most authentic version of yourself.

Choosing to 'go with the flow' means you get to live the life you were meant to live, instead of the default life of your predecessors. You switch the robot off and become human again, led by your soul. You step into yourself and take charge.

You get to be wild and free.

To break the mould. To return to your childlike innocence.

And by being 'you', you start to give those around you, permission to be more 'them' too. Your path lights the way for others to follow.

Some will, some won't.

That's one of the many challenges of this journey, but it's OK.

I've got you.

With this book as your source of inspiration, you will be able to flow through this incredible journey with spiritual arm bands on. This book will keep you afloat as you acquire the necessary knowledge and skills to embrace this new way of life.

OK, so....

What is Flow?

Let me give you one of my random experiences to bring it to life.

Flow is popping out to buy a coffee, a soya milk latte to be precise. With an idea in mind about where to buy it from, but all the while seeing an image of a food van floating in your mind's eye instead.

Surely not, you think?

When you get to the posh coffee shop you had intended to buy the coffee from, there's a huge queue and the food van next to it happens to have the exact milk you wanted and it's a fraction of the cost and wait for the coffee you had wanted. Win!

You're wearing what you think is the wrong coat (even though you had a strong feeling you had to wear it) because it is bloody freezing outside, but this coat happens to be so bright that it helps your friend to spot you walking along with your coffee, who needed a chat and some company just as much as you did.

The reality of Flow is that it is actually quite clunky.

But things do happen naturally and without the need to force or plan anything. By following what feels right, one step at a time, you naturally align with the right people, coffee, experience, opportunity, or whatever you need, at the right time.

It makes life the ultimate and never-ending surprise. Full of mini miracles that make you beam with joy.

You will be constantly re-directed and pleasantly confused by the outcome of any outing, situation, or experience. If you get out of the way and allow it to happen.

For example, you may get an intuitive hunch to go out for a walk, with a rough idea in mind of the route you will take. But when you step out of the door, it suddenly doesn't feel right, you are being guided elsewhere.

This is a wonderful moment of choice.

You can of course, stubbornly stick with your original plan that got you out of the house, or you can let the magic happen and follow your intuition. Your spiritual guidance. No matter how bizarre it may seem.

Here's another random story for you.

One morning, I had finished my honey. I realised it was Manuka honey which had travelled all the way from New Zealand. I made a vow to myself in that moment to only ever buy local honey in future.

I later went out for a walk and I thought I was going to find some beautiful nature to enjoy. However, I was being guided around the back streets of a residential area. I was walking along feeling a strong pull but with a confused look on my face. I was a little sulky for not getting what I wanted out of the walk if I'm honest. A bit of huffing and puffing on my part but I tried to remain open and curious.

I ended up in a cul-de-sac which looked like a dead end. Then something made me turn my head to the left and there was a sign saying, 'local honey'.

I am getting all the truth tingles as I write this.

It was a moment of magic. My jaw dropped to the floor, and I couldn't help but smile and laugh.

There was my local honey! No Google or sat nav required, just my instincts. I was amazed!

The intuitive mind rarely makes any logical sense.

The trick is not to question it. Most of the time you will not know, or understand, why you are being guided to do something. It's not for you to understand, in the moment at least, later it will make sense, it's just for you to follow and trust. You will be rewarded.

Maybe you would have had an equally nice walk if you had followed the path you had intended to go? Or maybe it would have been pretty standard instead of pretty magical?

Flow is choosing the magical over the mundane.

It's responding to the ever-changing signals of your body. Moment to moment. Day by day. Minute by minute.

What worked for you yesterday, may not work for you today. You set yourself a daily routine but your body has other needs and ideas the following day, or week or month.

Respond to the adjustment. The new knowledge. Let the old you go. This is OK, you are not a failure.

You are an intuitive being. Not a robot.

Trust that your body always knows best. It knows what it needs. But it only knows what it needs in the now.

Even if what you had going on was something that was 'good for you', like a run or morning yoga. If your body starts saying no. It's a no. Listen and honour it as the divine vessel of infinite wisdom that it is.

If you are connected with your body it will always tell you exactly what it needs and wants, in the moment. You may experience guilt around this.

For example, today I woke-up and I wanted chocolate and coffee for breakfast, in bed. Not the healthiest of choices but it's what made me happy that morning. I don't do that every morning but when I want to, I do!

You may not always be able to give your body exactly what it is asking for but listening and responding the best you can is still a step in the right direction.

You will go from living life on autopilot to loving life on instincts, and all of the magical twists and turns that this will inevitably involve.

Going with the flow works on everything – the big stuff and the small day to day seemingly insignificant decisions. Each small decision is an opportunity to build this connection and to hone your skills. It is an important training ground to learn how your intuition works. Its own unique language and signals.

I encourage you to practise and test it out with the small 'low risk' stuff to build-up your trust and faith in the magic. Then when the time comes, you will naturally feel more comfortable applying it to the bigger things in life.

Ok, I'm interested but what do I need to know, to flow?

Well, luckily for you, I have developed a philosophy for you to follow... let me introduce...

The Flow Philosophy.

The FLOW Philosophy

Through much trial and error, I discovered that 'going with the flow' has four distinct stages of skill development and learning. Each stage carries equal importance. There is no skipping a stage or trying to brush over it. To fully flow you need to learn how to embrace the challenges and gifts of all four of them.

So, what are the four stages, skills and knowledge you need to acquire in order to really flow?

Well, it's all in the word.

Faith

Leap

Open

Wait

I see it like an infinity symbol now. One side Yang (Faith and Leap) and the other Yin (Open and Wait).

Faith   Open

YANG   YIN

Leap   Wait

To complete a cycle, you must move through all 4 of the stages listed above. Each cycle will have a core lesson for you to learn. Ideally you don't want to keep repeating the same cycle (lessons) but you inevitably will.

The 'new' cycle may look different e.g., it will have different people, circumstances, etc but it will have the same core lesson for you to learn. If you complete a cycle mindfully using the flow philosophy you are less likely to keep repeating old habits.

But our core lessons have many layers to them so it may look like you are repeating a cycle sometimes, which can be frustrating, but it is actually slightly different. And with each cycle you go through, you are a different person, so you are never REALLY repeating a cycle just experiencing something similar as the new you.

How long does each cycle through the four stages last?

Well, that depends entirely on you and your own individual journey. You can speed through a cycle in a day, or you can sit stubbornly in one stage for months, or even years! It's always your choice.

Sometimes you can be in a long slow cycle, other times, short fast ones. Like the cycles on a washing machine – sometimes it's a quick wash, other times it's a slow old gentle eco wash that seems to go on FOREVER. You won't know what the length of the cycle is until it has finished, and you are looking back on it.

Sometimes there are smaller cycles within bigger cycles affecting different areas of your life.

The length of each stage of the cycle varies too. They are not all the same length in each cycle. And you can keep flipping back and forth between a couple of the stages before you can move through it.

Transitioning Between Stages

Just as you start to master and surrender to a particular stage it miraculously changes into the next.

That's how flow goes. It's always moving and changing.

The transition between the Yang and Yin mode can be the most challenging.

One minute you are flowing along getting shit done at the speed of lightning (Yang) then you are ground to a halt (Yin). This is infuriating (for me at least!). You are being asked to slow down, stop, integrate and process what you have already achieved and learned. It's a gift really to recharge, but in our society 'doing nothing' isn't really acceptable.

BUT, you can make it acceptable for yourself. Do it despite what other people think or feel about it. That's their stuff not yours. But it may well trigger your stuff too. That's why it is important to honour any guilt that comes up or frustration, anger, or whatever else it causes you to feel. This is an essential part of the process too.

Remember, this is you bravely choosing to step-up and out of your comfort zone. To do things your way, not the way you have been programmed to do them.

To do life differently. Living life on your terms.

It can actually become very uncomfortable in your 'comfort zone', but most people seem to be able to tolerate that for much longer.

Why? Because it's the known vs the unknown. The unknown seems so scary, and the known is well, known. It feels safe and predictable, at least we know what we are getting.

So...Why Flow?

What if the unknown was a super exciting spiritual pathway perfectly designed for your enjoyment and soul's growth? How could you say no to that?

It's a no brainer. Let's go!

FAITH

Flow starts by developing some form of faith. This doesn't have to be of the religious sort, but it can be.

Faith for me just means believing in something bigger than yourself, beyond the physical reality of the 3D world. It could be God, Goddess, love, your higher self, the Universe, higher power, Archangels, intuition, spirit guides, you name it. Literally, you get to choose whatever resonates with you. This is not a prescriptive thing.

It's just a case of opening your eyes to the unseen world, the felt world.

To realise that you are not alone, ever. You do not have to do this challenging life by yourself, without the support you need and deserve. You have a whole team of spiritual helpers who have been assigned the roles of assisting you on your path. Ask for their help and they will gladly act upon your invitation. But this help is not a passive thing, you don't get to rest on your laurels and have everything taken care of for you, unfortunately. You must act on any guidance you receive, despite it being super daunting at times.

But you have free will; you can choose to ignore the guidance or trust and follow it. This support and guidance are the most loving and pure kind, from entities that know you, and your purpose, deeply.

You will only ever be asked to do what they know you are capable of and can cope with at any given time. That's why spiritual guidance is drip-fed to us. We don't get the full picture, just a tiny piece of it at a time so as not to overwhelm us.

This spiritual connection will take some time to fully develop and learn to trust. The more you can carve out time and space to dedicate to a spiritual practice and learning to commune, the more in alignment you will become.

Flow always begins with checking-in with your faith of choice, because without it, it is unlikely that you will know what action to take at the next stage.

How do I know if I have Faith?

Faith is...

- Following your spiritual guidance or intuition, no matter how bonkers it may seem.

- Trusting that you will always have everything you need, but only when you actually need it.

- Surrendering to the unknown, again and again and again (this is hard!).

- Bravely letting go of that which no longer serves you – people, possessions, places, job roles, and the rest...with gratitude for what it taught you and the good times you did share.

- Believing in the magic of endings always leading to new and better beginnings.

- Calling on your spiritual helpers for anything and everything, big and small.

- Listening to your own personal connection to yourself and your faith above and beyond anyone else's opinions and advice.

- Knowing that even the 'bad' stuff is actually happening for your benefit.

- Not giving-up at the first hurdle but constantly demonstrating your faith by taking the necessary actions to move forward.

- Letting go of your plans, ideas, desired outcomes and welcoming in the surprise outcome you could not even have dreamed of.

- Knowing on a deep soul level that all is well, despite external appearances!

Skills Required:

Curiosity and an open mind.

Mode of Being:

Yang (fast paced, taking inspired action)

Astrology Element:

Air (Gemini, Libra, Aquarius)

The Element of Air in Astrology is about mindset, communication, curiosity, questioning, listening and learning.

These are the skills needed to acquire your Faith.

In this stage, it's important to re-program your mind, or to educate yourself. To find <u>your</u> truth. What makes sense to you. To question what you have been told and conditioned to believe and to start asking your own questions. It's time to find your own answers.

Follow your natural interests. The things you feel drawn to. Sign-up to a course or workshop. Buy that book. Go to that talk. Listen to that podcast. Watch that show or film even.

There may just be the smallest nugget of insight which opens your mind to a whole new way of experiencing the world. Or the perfect person on that course to connect with at this stage of your journey.

Tarot Card – The High Priestess

The High Priestess card is about connecting back in with your deep inner knowing and spiritual gifts. It wasn't safe in the past to use or share these freely, but we are living in very different times now. We can come out of the spiritual closest and embrace the magic once more. There are many tools to do this, Tarot just being one of them. Explore your natural interests. Get quiet and listen. Ask questions. Allow yourself to learn and experiment. Try different types of divination and notice which one brings you the most joy. Find or create a sacred space for you to do this. Somewhere peaceful where you will not be disturbed.

Planet – Jupiter

Big joyful Jupiter is as happy as he is wise, he's the sage of the zodiac. He knows his own philosophy of life and how to be authentic. He knows how to laugh at the ridiculous amount of fear there is to see through. He is the eternal optimist, the student and big-time lover of life. Never settling for what he has been told but discovering for himself his own truths and wisdom through experience and study. Asking the big questions – who am I? Why am I here? What is the purpose of this human existence?

Season – Spring

Spring is a very hopeful time of year. There is the promise of things to come, a fresh start, a spring in your step. New growth, a new year begins at springtime if you ask me. We've made it through the long cold winter and now we are ready to come out of the dark and into the light once more. But it still takes time for new growth to show itself. It requires action – sowing seeds. Letting them grow in the right conditions. Nurturing new ideas.

Channelled Message:

We are always here. Do not worry. Stay strong in your faith. Believe you can. Do not let naysayers convince you otherwise. You are connected to something greater than that which you can see. You feel it, sense it, know it but there is no physical evidence. Only through experience can you build your own evidence and spiritual strength. It will come and go, when you feel disconnected, we are still there but we want you to have 'you' time to figure things out for yourself. We help when we can. We do, we love you and we want only the best for you. You will encounter challenges with or without our support but please know that it is always for your benefit in the long run. We know how strong and capable you are, and it is within these challenges that you rise from the ashes stronger than ever. See the difficulties as opportunities to rise up.

How to Cultivate Faith:

Your Faith is yours to discover, I found mine in a particular way (more on this in Part 2) but please be open to finding yours in whatever way feels most joyful for you. Following what lights you up will always take you the right way. Here are some of my suggestions but feel free to find your own:

• Read inspiring books (recommendations included).

- Connect with Tarot Cards or book a tarot reading (more on this later).

- Have an Astrology reading or learn more about it (see section on this).

- Dowsing (more on this later).

- Make time to meditate.

- Practice yoga, tai chi, or something similar.

- Connect with like-minded people, learn from them.

- Follow your joy.

- Visit spiritual places.

- Take some time to be still and silent.

- Spend time in nature.

Journaling: Be Honest with Yourself

At the end of each section of FLOW I will share some journal prompts to help you to examine and explore the tough stuff.

Come back to these questions as often as you need to. They will help you to understand why you are feeling the way you are feeling. The answers may shift and change over time or you may spot a recurring pattern.

Start with the questions you find easy and work your way up to the ones that seem scary.

In my experience, you are likely to get stuck and feel very strong emotions at the same stage of flow each time. Some stages you will sail through and enjoy, others you will resist and find super challenging. Sometimes you might battle with them all, that's OK.

We all have our sore spots, but which one is yours?

My advice is to lean into it. Fully go there. Dig around in all the things you have been hiding from. Ask yourself the difficult questions and be really honest with your answers. You will feel loads better for doing it, be brave my flow friend.

Suggestion:

Buy a beautiful journal or notebook that makes you smile and represents Flow for you.

Get to writing like a curious child.

Journal Prompts:

On a scale of 1-10, what is your current level of faith?

How does this number make you feel?

How could it be different?

What is your daily practice to connect with something higher than you?

How do you feel when you take the time to do this?

What else could you do? Or would you like to do?

How could you make time for this?

Where and when do you feel most connected?

What did this section bring up for you? Honour every emotion – were you excited, irritated, angry or happy? Name it and write about it, it has something to teach you.

LEAP

There is probably something in your life that is causing you a lot of stress or grief right now. It could be your job, your home, your relationship, your lifestyle, your strict routine or lack thereof, your health, your belongings, family, or anything else.

These things are happening to get your attention. To get you to notice that something isn't quite right and for you to take action to change things.

You may be avoiding making a change that you know deep down is absolutely necessary. Perhaps you are finding clever ways to justify why you can't possibly make that change over and over again.

Maybe you are stuck in a rut of your own making, that you just can't seem to see a way out of?

But here's the deal, once you have developed faith you then need to act on it. Faith without action, isn't faith at all. By avoiding taking the necessary action to relieve your current problems or symptoms you are saying, 'I don't trust the universe to support me'. That's not faith, that's fear.

If, however, you can find the courage and strength to make the change that you already know needs to happen, you will be actively demonstrating your faith. This is sending a whole new message out to the universe. It says – "OK, I trust you, I know you will catch me. Even though I can't see the path ahead or the full plan. I know it is there and I will take the first step with my eyes closed."

Making the change will not be easy but staying where you are is a whole lot harder. And it will get more and more uncomfortable until you do something about it. Because the change is important for your growth and the universe is pushing you to go for it. It's like the rug slowly being pulled from beneath your feet. It feels unsettling and you want to cling to that rug for dear life, but that rug just isn't for you anymore. It's time to let it go.

Now, you may, or may not, have supporters around you. You will definitely have people around you who think your idea to change something is a bad one. Maybe it's never been done that way before or it seems illogical to them. Maybe they think you are being ungrateful or thinking the grass is greener. That's their experience, not yours. Trust yourself. Do what feels right for you. Do it your way.

Follow your own internal guidance. Despite the naysayers!

This is exhilarating.

When travelling around New Zealand at 18 years old, I did a bungee jump. I always knew it was something I wanted to do, and this was my opportunity. I had a plan. I would get to the end of the ledge and jump after the count of 3.

I feel nervous re-living this moment. It was agonising. I stood on the end of the ledge and froze with fear.

How could I jump into thin air? This was madness! My body quickly responded to the fear in my mind. The longer I stood there trying to 'psyche' myself up, the more fear I felt. My body went numb.

The guy that worked there said, "The longer you stand there the harder it gets and the less likely you are to jump." He kept talking to me to distract my thoughts. The crowds were shouting my name. This did not help. It added pressure and I couldn't hear myself think.

The guy started to pull the bungee cord back up to make way for someone else to jump. This made me more determined. I knew that I wanted to do this and if I didn't do it now, I would have to go through this whole saga again at another time. It was a gruelling 7 minutes before I jumped, but I did it.

Falling was actually the easy bit. I felt amazingly free and a huge sense of relief. Jumping into thin air with water beneath me was absolutely terrifying.

I'm sharing this story to illustrate that the thought of the leap is worse than the actual leap itself and the longer you stall or put it off the more uncomfortable you feel.

Skills Required:

A shit load of courage and a whole lot of faith.

Mode of Being:

Yang (fast paced, taking inspired action)

Astrology Element:

Fire (Aries, Leo, Sagittarius)

Fire is about creativity, passion, excitement, courage, action, movement, and change.

When your inner fire is burning bright you feel like you can do anything. Think about what ignites your inner fire? What makes you feel strong, connected and powerful? It could be dancing, singing, or running. It could be creating, cooking, or painting.

First begin by lighting yourself back up. Experiment with what brings you joy and makes you feel alive. What did you enjoy doing as a child? Reconnect with your child-like sense of fun and do that.

You can also connect directly with the element of fire by doing a letting go ritual. To burn that which no longer serves you. It may be a list that you write of things that you are ready to release from your life. Or old diaries or love notes that keep you tied to the past and are stopping you from moving forward.

Before I left for Bali, I did a lot of Kali style burning ceremonies. Kali is the Goddess of endings and new beginnings.

While on a walk with a friend, she mentioned that she had boxes and boxes of diaries from childhood that she was ready to let go of. I had a chiminea and suggested we do it together. I began the search for things I could burn to support her.

We set the scene with a glass of fizz and invoked Kali with some incense. We stayed up until the early hours of the morning burning through those diaries.

I had found old course notes, travel scrapbooks and journals, even my 1st class dissertation went on the fire! I realised that none of those things represented the real me. Yes, I had a lot of fun on my travels and at Uni but I am totally different person now and I was ready for my new chapter to begin. I didn't want to keep re-reading the old books, I wanted to write a new one. I released anything anchoring me to a past that no longer felt authentic and unnecessarily weighing me down.

The power of this ceremony was quite remarkable. My friend who had been living in a shared house her whole adult life quickly found the courage to put in an offer on a home of her own within a couple of weeks of letting go of her past. She had spent almost 2 years troubled by this decision and suddenly it flowed with ease.

Tarot Card – The Fool

This card requires you to jump before you can see the next step. To find your inner child like trust in the magic of the Universe to support you, no matter what. One part of you will be super excited by this, and another will be petrified. That's OK. It's normal and natural to feel scared when making any change. It's about riding the waves of fear and excitement and just taking the plunge anyway. No-one can do this for you. The anticipation and decision-making process is the most agonising part. The leap feels super empowering when you finally do it.

Planet – Uranus

Uranus is the freedom lover, the rebel, the 'don't tell me what to do' part of us. It is the ultimate risk taker of the zodiac. It wants to jump out of the box it was once put into. It wants to smash up that box and find its own way without any bloody boxes. Who needs a box anyway? Its energy offers the opportunity of quick and sudden change. Freedom of movement and choice. Breaking out of convention and into the life that will bring you the most joy.

Season - Summer

We have a lot of energy and excitement for life in summertime. Days are long and much can be achieved. This is the time to take inspired action. It's a naturally optimistic time of year, so ride on that sunshine. Be brave, muster up the courage and jump into the unknown.

Please note...it doesn't have to be the actual summer season for you to leap but I am offering this explanation to further enhance your understanding of each stage of the cycle.

Channelled Message:

It is time to act on your faith. This is scary but necessary – you can do it. The fear is there to protect you, but you do not need protecting. You know in your heart of hearts when something is no longer right for you, it is time for change. Do not focus on the loss, although you will need to grieve, focus on what you could gain from taking this brave step into the unknown. Leaving what you don't want, makes space for the new. Something better is on the horizon even if you cannot see what it is. Trust and you will see. Do not live in fear. Take action and you will be supported.

How to Leap

Yes, you are stuck between a rock and a hard place, or so it seems.

You are the rock that needs to be dropped into the ocean of possibilities. We all know how satisfying that feels. Throwing a big rock into the ocean.

It's a choice you are making every single day, over and over again. To stay where you are. To suffer and struggle. Or you can try a new way. A magical way.

Remember when you believed in magic as a child? That hopeful child still lives inside you, shrouded by years of lies, and the conditioning received from others and society. This child is begging for your attention. For you to trust in magic again.

To open a new door. But to open this new door, you must close the old one. You can't leave it ajar, that's not faith in action. That's hedging your bets and the universe doesn't play that game.

Do whatever you can to make the change easier for yourself. Can you ask for help and support from others? Do you need a mentor? Or an Astrology reading? Maybe some healing sessions? Maybe you just need to work on boosting your faith more? Check in with yourself about what you would need to feel safer to make the change. Give that to yourself.

Is it to calm your own fears or is it someone else's fear that you've inherited? Are you worried about what people might think or how they will react?

Find a way to let go of the things that are blocking you from moving forward. It will be worth it.

What Happens If I Don't Leap?

OK, so you have free will. It's your choice to leap or not.

BUT, if you don't leap, the universe may just push you. I'm not saying this to scare you but if you are not learning your lessons, the universe will help you along the way.

This feels like a 'Tower' moment in the Tarot deck. When suddenly your world seems to fall apart, things are taken away from you so that you have to make that change that you have been so desperately avoiding. This can be a redundancy, a devastating break-up, being forced to move from where you are or a health problem. These things, despite appearances, are happening for your benefit. The universe wants better for you and if you cannot see that it will start to nudge you in the right direction.

I have had many a Tower moment in my life, even though I am a natural leaper! Sometimes I just want to cling to what I have and stop going through changes or trusting in the unknown. It's bloody tiring and I often think, "I deserve a bloody break"– so I try and dig my heels in. This doesn't work.

The shake-up always happens one way or another and it's much nicer when it's on your terms, let me tell you.

Examples of my Tower moments are:

- During my Saturn Return, which is a big time for 'Tower' moments, if you are not learning your lessons. I was made redundant from an employed position, which prompted me to make the transition to being self-employed. This was really stressful and a major challenge in my life but most definitely the best thing for me. I never enjoyed having a boss anyway, I'm a Leo!

- Being given notice on my flat that I had only been in for 3 months in my attempt to 'settle down' for the first time in a long time. I was in such denial of this that I recycled the letter and pretended it wasn't happening. I thought I could beg my way out of it with the angels! But that didn't work. Luckily, another flat turned up, with less than 2 weeks to spare. The flat ended up being less than ideal BUT this then prompted me to write my third book. It also helped me to realise what I want and don't want from a place to live.

- Having the worst house-sitting experience ever (don't ask!) – which was a sign that I needed to stop and start living differently.

- Not having the man, I thought I wanted to return my affections and for him to brutally call it off with me. This has happened more than once!!!

When I was going through these things it was absolutely horrendous. I hated the universe for doing it to me, I felt sorry for myself, I wanted to give-up and just live a 'normal' life, whatever that is. But I didn't, I kept going and trying to see the blessing in disguise of a shit situation. But you often need to be out of the storm and for the dust to settle before you can see it clearly.

After a few experiences like the above, you start to notice the early warning signs and prepare yourself to take action. I knew, for example, that it was time to leave my second flat after only 3 months of being there again. How did I know? Because I had a very noisy neighbour! This is the way that the universe prods you to make a change – by making you increasingly uncomfortable. At first, I wrote a polite note to the neighbour and it got better for a bit, then it got really bad. My breaking point was when I was woken up at 7am on a Sunday morning by them running on their treadmill, which was above my bedroom, with their T.V blasting out. This lit my inner fire! I literally saw red.

This time, I wrote another more strongly worded note and delivered it with some very loud knocks on their door, then I reported it to my landlord and the management company and handed-in my notice. This felt so good! I was standing up for myself and moving on to better things. I had no idea where I was going and how it was all going to happen, but I started to prepare by decluttering, and I trusted the right place would show up at the right time for me. The neighbour wasn't a problem after I had taken the action. It was tempting to back track and stay where I was, but I still knew I needed to leave, that was just my shove to do something about it.

It was only a week until I had to move that the new place appeared, I kept it from my family until this point as I didn't want to worry them, and this was very stressful! But my next place did show-up and it was definitely the right move.

Journal Prompts:

How does hearing about other people taking a leap of faith feel for you? Are you jealous or judgemental? Are you inspired or intrigued? Ask why.

Have you already taken your leap? Or are you stalling?

Do you know what your leap is? What if you did know?

Recall a time when you did make a big change in the past, how did it feel both before, during and after?

What made you finally do it? How did you find the courage?

How did the people around you react?

What is stopping you from leaping?

What do you fear would happen if you let go of what isn't right for you?

What if things went well for you? What is the best-case scenario?

Do you trust yourself to make the right decision? If not, why?

How would it feel to be free of the burden you carry?

Imagine you've already leaped – how does it feel? What is different?

Have you experienced a Tower moment? What was it? How did it benefit you?

OPEN

After the initial leap of faith, you get bumped back down to reality. Life is life after all.

Yes, you will feel lighter for not having the burden you were carrying weighing you down any longer. And you may still be experiencing the high of finally taking empowering action. But now you have new challenges and fears coming up. Self-doubt kicks in big time and the grief for what you no longer have.

This does not mean you have done the wrong thing. It is a sign that you have successfully stepped out of your comfort zone and into something new. This will inevitably bring up a lot of emotions.

Being open means being open to everything. The good and the bad. That means you need to be open to feeling ALL of it. The fear, the upset, the anger, the rage, the grief, the shock, the guilt, the hopelessness, the self-pity, the self-doubt, whatever you are feeling. If you are flowing right you will feel all of this and more.

This is good. These painful feelings need to be felt. You have attracted the current situation you are dealing with in your life to probe your sore spots. They need probing, even if it is bloody painful. Feeling the feelings will crack you open in a messy and exhausting yet beautiful way. This is necessary for you to go through, to make space to fully receive and feel more love, support, guidance and healing.

If you try and block or avoid the tough stuff, you do not get to experience the endless stream of abundance and love that is waiting to pour through you.

I'll give you a real-life example...

I was supposed to be on a date this afternoon, but I cancelled it. I had already had a phone call with the guy, and I was picking-up on some early warning signs that he wasn't for me. We had good banter but fundamentally we were very different people. He had a very busy schedule which mostly consisted of work and exercise. I sensed that we do and see life very differently.

I've been in relationships like that in the past and it just doesn't work for me. I could have gone for a 'green tea' with him as he suggested and a walk, but it didn't excite me. I preferred the thought of spending the afternoon writing. I decided to let him know how I was feeling and to call the date off. He respected my decision.

So now I am sad, the promise of a date and someone to flirt with has gone and I am now firmly back in 'no man land'. I don't have any other options on the table at the moment and I feel lonely and sad.

I'm crying as I write this now. I started to question my decision, thinking, "Oh shit, what have I done?" Maybe I jumped to conclusions too soon, maybe I should have at least gone on one date. But deep down I know I did the right thing and to backtrack might save some pain in the short term, but it could create more pain in the long term.

Yes, my spiritual self knows I won't be alone forever, but my human self is fed-up of waiting and longing for something which never shows up. As I write this, I am allowing the tears to flow. I have to, to make space for the new.

But easy come, easy go. I don't mean that in a heartless way. It's just something worth reminding yourself of. Things show up in your life 'out of the blue' – one minute you are alone, the next you meet someone. But just because they came into your life with ease doesn't mean you need to keep them. Some people come and go quickly, but we can still learn from them.

I'm proud of myself for trusting my feelings and choosing to walk away when I did. But even when it is the 'right' thing to do for yourself, it still hurts, and you doubt your decision.

Just four days later I connected with a new guy who was an upgrade. I didn't know he was on the horizon, or when he would arrive, I just had to follow what felt right and trust that something else would arrive when the time was right. And so, another cycle begins.

You may only need a day or two to feel what you are feeling, I like to do it in a dramatic and intense way, but you do. But please find a way to grieve the loss or to get angry about the injustice or just have a 'feel sorry for me day' – it's essential that you do make time and space for this because...

Before the breakthrough, there is always a BREAKDOWN.

I am reminded of the song 'What a difference a day makes, 24 little hours'. Honestly, one day you can be in the depths of despair and the next day you finally have the clarity you have so desperately been seeking. You have to clear the emotions blocking clarity for it to come. There is no other way through.

But make sure you are crying about the real thing, which is often not the thing you think it is. The current thing is just a reminder of a past pain you have felt and not yet released. That is why it is showing up in a different form for you to take another look at.

Sometimes when your emotions are involved it is super hard to see clearly – talk to a friend, family member or better still someone neutral like a therapist, healer or trusted psychic to help you get to the root of your pain so you can really dig it out.

Sometimes you have to look back before you can move forward.

This is something I have noticed about flow life. Sometimes, you can't help but sneak a peek at an old door before you are really ready to move forward. You might just open it briefly and have a quick glance around to remind yourself of why you shut it in the first place. Or you might go in the door, to re-experience it or get some form of closure or confirmation that you did the right thing, before you can fully let it go. That's OK, do what you need to do but try and be mindful that it is happening.

I usually do this when I am scared to move forward and not sure of what is coming. Or I feel I may have been too hasty with letting go. Or impatient for the new to arrive!

During the Yin phases of Flow, there's not a lot going on, so you start to panic and try to backtrack. But it doesn't take long to remember why you walked away from something when you attempt to re-visit it. And you often see it more clearly after some time and distance apart.

I'll give you an example.

I've done this a lot with career changes. I let something go because it feels right to do so, like my Tarot readings but then I miss it a bit and idealise how it was to do them. I start to think I could do it again and when I try, it either doesn't flow or I don't enjoy it like I once did.

It's the same with friendships, I let someone go because I do not feel like we are vibing like we once were. It feels like we are playing different music and can't hear each other anymore. I miss what we once had and try to reconnect on occasion, but the problem still exists. We are at very different stages of our journey and I was right to walk away.

Be aware that friends you have outgrown might not agree with your decision or understand why you need to walk away, but by doing what is best for you, you are ultimately doing what is best for them too. Sometimes it's mutual, sometimes it's not.

Skills Required:

Plenty of sob your heart out sessions.

Permission to be human.

Mode of Being:

Yin (very slow-paced doing, lots of self-care, feeling your emotions, receptive to support and guidance).

Astrology Element:

Water (Cancer, Scorpio, Pisces).

Flow is not just about water, but it is a very important part of it.

Water is about our deep emotions, sensitivity, receptivity, going inwards, retreating, silence, stillness, nurturing, gentleness, and feeling.

There is great wisdom in our emotions – they are our greatest teachers and yet we brush them aside or try to justify them with logic and reason. We've been taught that emotions are annoying inconveniences when in fact they are gold dust.

Tune in and feel the feelings. Let them pass through you. Cry for your loss. Cry for your inner child.

Cry for your adult self. Cry for having to suppress all of that for so long.

We all have a backlog of emotions to work through. Stored pain, trauma, upset, anger etc. The body holds it all until we fully feel it.

Emotions quickly pass when you let them flow as they are meant to. Like a child having a tantrum – they do it in the moment, they feel it all there and then, and then they move on.

We are still children. With crazy strong emotions but we have been conditioned to believe this is no longer true. Only children can throw a tantrum or get so upset they cannot breathe. This is simply not true.

Yes, we have developed a certain level of maturity, but we are still childlike at our core. We need to get good at honouring and parenting our inner child (ourselves) in the way we wish we were as a child.

Compassion, kindness, forgiveness starts with you. It's so easy to blame others for what you did not receive. But maybe they didn't get it either? Maybe this all happened so that one day you will learn to give it to yourself and break the cycle for future generations.

Tarot Card – Temperance

To fully open you must allow your emotions to flow. No matter how hard they are to experience. This is a time to get really honest with yourself about how you are feeling and what is bothering you.

What has come up for you now that you have taken your leap of faith? No matter how big or small. Standstill and tune in. You need to stop and get off the merry-go-round of busy-ness to fully acknowledge the way you are feeling.

We are often taught to brush over our emotions, or try to justify or minimise them, but that is a great disservice to ourselves. They are our greatest teacher, and they lead the way to our deepest healing. By allowing our emotions to be felt and honoured they pass through us and are healed. Get the tissues ready. Have a good cry about anything and everything and trust me you will feel better for doing it. Even if the same old stuff comes up time and time again. Which it will because there are many complex layers to our emotional patterns and behaviours. Trust that you are making progress and releasing it all bit by bit.

Planet – Pluto

Deep healing and transformation are the name of the game for my mate, Pluto. He gets a bad reputation, but he should not be feared. Emotions are not good or bad, they are part of being human, whether you like it or not. When we allow ourselves to dig deep and feel what needs to be felt it is the best feeling. Not during, but after the release!

The energy of Pluto brings the dark to the light to be seen, felt and witnessed. All the hurt you've stuffed down because it felt too much to deal with doesn't go away, it just sits there festering and waiting for you to tend to it. You will karmically draw problems into your life which trigger the emotions you are suppressing, as a way for them to get your attention. The sooner you do the healing work, the sooner you can break the cycle.

Season – Autumn

Trees shed their leaves in autumn – the leaves are like tears falling. They let go of so many leaves, until they are bare. They instinctively know how and when to do this. They let what has become old leave to make way for the new growth that wants to happen. But they know it is not immediate. Some leaves are harder to let go of than others, sometimes the wind blows, and lots fall at the same time. The tree doesn't force the leaves to fall, it just allows it to happen.

Channelled Message

We feel your pain and we want you to feel it too. It needs you to be fully present with it. Learn from it and heal old wounds. These wounds will mainly stem from childhood, some will be connected to past lives and ancestral patterns. It can feel very dark during these times, very dark indeed. Danielle has been through many painful crying days and nights, after the sky is blue again. You feel lighter and cleansed. Stay with the pain, let it pass through, be kind and gentle with yourself.

How to Open

Remember the corridor time.

You can't close one door and head straight into the next. That is logistically impossible.

It may be tempting to jump right back into the old door, or quickly open another door that you know will just be more of the same old crap. Don't. It's not for you. It will just delay your freedom and progress and be something else you will need to eventually let go of. Hold your nerve. You've got this.

When one door is closed properly, another one, a much better one, will always open. This may take some time to appear. Often you can't fully see the new door before you leap, but it's there. Keep the faith.

This is a precious and important time to process your loss, to grieve what you have bravely let go of.

Whenever we choose to walk away from something or someone that wasn't right for us. No matter what the circumstances - you will experience grief, pain, loss, anger, upset, frustration, disappointment, all of it. Pain is an important part of the process of letting go. That pain needs to be released to make space for more love and happiness. The sooner you allow yourself to feel all the upset, the sooner you open the floodgates to more joy and abundance.

But you have to be open to receive the abundance that wants to come to you.

Opportunities and support may come your way from new avenues. Ones that you would normally say no to. You are likely to be asked to receive in a different way. You don't get to choose how and when you receive. You can't say, "Well I'm comfortable with earning my own money so I will only receive in that way," when the universe is handing you a free ride, but it involves letting someone else support you for a while.

Change brings up our blocks to receiving.

Start by creating space to feel. Quiet time, without constant noise and distractions. We are all so scared to be with ourselves. To be alone. We surround ourselves with people and things and constant doing. This is to avoid feeling.

Feeling bored, uncomfortable, emotional, sad, angry, frustrated. Whatever. These feelings have to be felt before they can move on. Before you can move on.

Stop and pay attention. Ask your body to show you what it is feeling. You may get a weird pain or sensation in your chest. Then suddenly a memory pops into your head from childhood. Write about it. Connect with it. Give it the time and space that it needs to be processed. Have a cry if you need to. Notice if you find it difficult to cry. Ask why? When did you learn this?

This is super hard and scary at first but the more you do it, the better you will feel. Start with just a little daily check in if you can and then work up to some longer periods of sitting with your feelings.

Feel it, to heal it. And then you are free.

Opening can be extremely draining on all levels- emotional, physically and spiritually. You have to be REALLY gentle with yourself while you are going through this stage. Treat yourself how you would treat an upset child- be kind, loving and understanding.

Journal Prompts:

Do you feel your emotions or do you think them?

How could you feel them? Where are they held in your body? Just notice and breathe.

Are you able to cry?

When was the last time you properly cried about something?

What song or film helps you to tap into your emotions?

How do you feel when you receive help, support or love from others?

Are you open to feeling and expressing your difficult emotions like pain, upset, anger, rage, frustration, hopelessness?

Which emotions are harder for you to admit to yourself?

How do you make time and space for processing challenging emotions? What soothes you?

Can you ask for help?

WAIT

Flow doesn't always mean movement.

You don't get to jump into this magical stream and be swept along for the rest of your life with ease and grace. This would be far too easy and would allow for zero soul growth.

Waiting is about trusting in divine timing.

There is a plan, but a lot of it happens behind the scenes. Certain things need to line up before you are nudged to take your next step. This can feel like you are being kept in a holding pen or held in the dark. You sense something is going on, but you can't see it.

It's the same feeling when a surprise is being planned for you. You feel left out and nervous about what it is. You want to know what's going on.

You won't know what's going on. You need to get comfortable with the unknown. This is the time to surrender and focus on self-care.

You will never be expected to keep leaping. This is an exhausting emotional process. Letting go of anything requires grieving time and rest. Focus on the things you can do to make yourself feel better, not what you can't. This can be as simple as getting on top of your laundry, or clearing out a cupboard that's been bothering you, having a duvet day, binge watching a good boxset, pampering yourself or doing some batch cooking. Indulge yourself, this is your reward for opening!

You close one door, and you must wait in the corridor for a while before opening the next door. You may feel there are no doors to open and you are left in a blank room with nothing to do. Some of the doors are cleverly concealed from sight. If you knew the whole plan your mind would go crazy trying to figure out the 'how' and mess it all up.

Fill your corridor up with enjoyable things. Try to relax and enjoy yourself. Waiting is letting the universe take over for a while.

Get out of the way. For me, this stage is often my greatest challenge, I fight against it EVERY time. I'm an impatient fireball and waiting does not sit well with me.

It happened yesterday; I had a total meltdown about not having finished this book yet. It feels like it's dragged on for ages and I just want it FINISHED already but it wasn't flowing. I wallowed in my own self-pity, had a chat with my Mum about it (I actually shouted, "I JUST WANT IT FUCKING FINISHED!" during this call, sorry Mum!) and sulked the day away.

At this point I could do nothing but give up trying to make something happen and surrender to whatever the book wanted me to do, if it wasn't the time to write there was obviously a good reason for it.

But today I woke up feeling energised and inspired again. I clearly had some blocked emotions stopping the creative process from flowing and I needed a rest day. Note to self – read your own bloody book when this happens again!

Rest, recuperate, integrate what has already happened, recharge your batteries. This is important preparation time for what comes next. Relax and enjoy the downtime, if you aren't being guided to do anything then do nothing.

This can be difficult because we have been programmed to be 'productive doers' but this is about 'being still'. There will be guilt around this but do it anyway and feel your way through the guilt.

Prioritise sleep, take as many naps as you need, long walks in nature, read, write, spend time alone, develop new skills, heal anything that is being triggered (more on this later). Nourish your body and mind. This is a holiday, it's a reward for what you have already achieved. Accept the treat and enjoy it.

The more you fight against it, the longer you will be waiting.

Skills Required:

Patience and non-resistance.

Mode of Being:

Yin (very slow-paced doing, lots of self-care, feeling your emotions, receptive to support and guidance)

Astrology Element:

Earth (Taurus, Virgo, Capricorn)

Earth is all about practical matters – cleaning, tidying, organising, cooking, routine, the five senses, structure, our to-do lists, nature, preparation, grounding, and slowing down.

After a fire the ground is regenerated for new growth, this can take some time. You can only plant seeds at the right time of year, when the soil is fertile again. You cannot rush or force this process.

Learn to enjoy being stuck in the mud. Take it slow and steady here. The pace has changed. Be kind and gentle with yourself. Do practical things at a snail's pace. Notice the sensations. The smells. The sounds. The textures. The Tastes.

Or do nothing. Personally, I like to get lost in a good boxset while I wait. It takes my mind off what I am waiting for and helps me to relax and enjoy my time off.

During this stage I would recommend lots of rest and home comforts. Things that bring you pleasure and make you feel safe and supported. You can write a list or start to notice the things in your life that need your attention and gently and methodically work your way through them. Only when it feels good to do so.

Trust that any delays or setbacks that you experience are happening for your benefit, even if you don't know why yet.

Remember, this is important preparation time for what is to come. You do not know what is coming, but it is, and you need to be ready for it so recharge the batteries and get your ducks in a row.

Tarot Card – The Hanged Man

This card is actually a good sign that something new is on the horizon and you need to prepare yourself for it. Don't go too mad 'doing stuff'. The pace of this stage is slow and steady. Doing things gently and allowing plenty of time for rest and recuperation in-between. Tend to the things that you noticed were bothering you in the open stage. Act on or plan to take care of what came up for you.

These things require your attention.

For me, it tends to be clearing out the old to make way for the new. Suddenly my home wants to be cleaned and organised. I see my belongings differently after a good emotional clear out. I am shedding my skin again.

At first, I was reluctant to let go as I didn't know what, if anything, was coming in to replace it. I know now with certainty, that the cycle of endings and new beginnings can be trusted completely. Now I let go and notice and write about any resistance to it. The more I am willing and able to let go of that which I am guided to, the more space I am making for the wonderful new stuff that is meant for me to come in. And it's always better than what I had.

Planet – Saturn

Saturn is about tending to the boring stuff. Your responsibilities, chores, to do list, day to day life. These are the things we sometimes put off but feel so much better for actually doing.

Saturn does not move fast. He takes his time, but he gets everything done, step by step, practical, methodical and hardworking. Use the time you have wisely. Write a list and no matter how much resistance you have to doing it, start chipping away, bit by bit. Stop and rest when you need to. Rome wasn't built in a day and all that.

The universe always allows you plenty of time to do whatever you need to do, it's us that adds unnecessary pressure and stress on an already perfectly planned timeline. Look after your body, home and finances when Saturn is knocking on your door.

Season – Winter

Winter is cold and dark (typically, in the UK at least). Short days. Hibernation mode kicks in. You want home comforts; nourishing food and we naturally slow down and do less. The trees are bare, there is very little colour in our lives. Some red berries around perhaps. The root chakra is calling. Trust in the stillness of this period to recharge, to know that the soil is being replenished for new growth. Spring will come again, but it takes time.

Channelled Message:

We do not want you to burn yourself out, it is as important to rest as it is to take action. Life is not meant to be stressful or lived in the fast lane. You always have plenty of time to do whatever you need to do. Taking care of yourself is important. Tend to your home, health and take your time with it. You cannot focus if you have a to-do list on your mind, we know this. You are a human as well as a spiritual soul. Tend to your basic human needs. Listen and respond to your body. Danielle spends a lot of time resting and then she is amazed at what she can achieve in a short period of time. If you feel sleepy or tired then nap, we often send energy upgrades, downloads and healing during your quiet periods. Rest to fully receive it.

How to Wait

Drop all of the 'shoulds'. 'Well, I should be doing this' or 'I should be doing that'. The only person who is actually 'shoulding' you, is you. You can try blaming as many people as you like for these 'shoulds' but ultimately, what you do or don't do is your choice. Always. But we forget this when we behave unconsciously.

We've all been programmed this way. To do what we have been told and then we don't even realise we are doing it. Allow yourself to rebel. To do what you REALLY want to do. Always do what FEELS good.

If it stresses you out, you are probably going the wrong way. Don't force yourself to do something, just because it seems like what needs to be done. Do it only when you feel it is right. There is a lot of guilt that comes up with living this way. Trust me, I spend most of my time watching T.V. in bed, it's how I do, what I do. It works for me; from the outside it looks like I'm a lazy bitch. Sometimes I feel like that too. I rest a LOT and then I have small spurts of energy to get on with things efficiently, then I rest some more. That's just the way I roll. You might be a slow and steady horse that wins the race, I am a sprinter who needs to recharge often. And carb load!

Give yourself permission to wait in a style that suits you. Stop fighting against time. You will only exhaust yourself. Let go and drift for a while. See where it takes you. What it teaches you. What gifts it has for you.

I often find that I am guided to clear the decks during this time. To declutter the physical items that my body had an emotional connection to. This makes space for the new to come in. I always have some resistance to letting these things go but I know that if I'm thinking about it, it is time.

You will always have everything you need, when you need it. Therefore, there is no need to cling to what you already have. There is always more. Letting it go with gratitude for what it has taught you, and how it made you feel for the time you owned it or had it in your life, honours this process.

Journal Prompts:

How do you respond to delays? Or setbacks?

Why do you want it all to happen now?

How could this downtime or delay be for your benefit?

How could you fully relax and enjoy this precious time?

What could you do to prepare yourself for when things do speed up again?

What is the rush?

Can you allow yourself to enjoy the simple pleasures of life, slowly?

If not, what does it bring up for you? Write about it.

What is stopping you from fully surrendering to the here and now?

What would it take for you to stop and do nothing on purpose?

What could you declutter or clean? Ask your home to show you what needs your attention first.

PART 2

Let's Get Realistic

How I Found Flow: My Story

I am sharing my story in all its glory to illustrate, with a real-life example, the flow philosophy in action, and how I came to develop it.

Please be mindful that what follows is only one example of how this can go.

On reflection, my story is pretty extreme. I'm a risk-taker. Leaping is easy for me. I have a lot of courage and I am optimistic by nature. Overly so, on occasion!

This is the way I did it. Do not try and copy my journey. Take from it what resonates or inspires you and leave the rest.

Your story will be very different to mine.

Flow is about discovering your own unique and authentic adventure back to you.

Looking back, if I could give myself one piece of advice, it would be...

Be gentle with yourself.

Finding my Faith

It was an ongoing health problem (ironically with my menstrual cycle – the ultimate flow!) which pushed me down the road of alternative therapies, and this soon became my catalyst for awakening.

I enrolled on a Kinesiology course and met a lot of spiritual people for the first time in my life.

I was amazed by the impact of this healing modality and started to offer taster sessions to my then hypnotherapy clients. I was working from my home office at the time.

Soon after, I started to notice a feeling of being claustrophobic in my house. I would get shivers up my spine when walking upstairs, like there was someone there but I couldn't see them. I would walk into the living room, with the doors and windows closed, and I would smell cigarette smoke. We were a non-smoking household. How could this be?

I spoke to one of my new spiritually minded friends about this. She had experienced something similar, with the energy of her home feeling a bit off and had called in a woman who could spiritually cleanse and protect the home.

I booked a session and the woman tuned in remotely to the house to see what was going on for me. I was a bit sceptical at this point but open enough to try it. I like to experience things for myself before I make up my mind about something.

She called me after the cleanse was complete to talk me through her findings. What she revealed was truly amazing. No wonder I felt like I couldn't breathe!

The house was full of spirits of immigrants who were connected to the tobacco trade. I was living very close to the old tobacco factory at the time. Unbeknownst to me, the spirits had entered the house along with my clients. I was like a shining light when doing my healing work and they thought I could help them to cross over.

Of course, at this stage I didn't know how to do this. I had no idea I was so energetically open. She cleared the spirits and protected the house from future uninvited guests. The house felt clear and fresh. I could breathe again. It felt noticeably lighter and brighter, and I had no more shivers up my spine.

This experience was a big eye opener to me about the 'unseen world' we share our space with. It reminded me of my childhood experiences of seeing and sensing things I could not understand, and nor could my parents, so it was quickly dismissed. This is the start of us not trusting our instincts. We are told there isn't anything there, nothing to worry about. It isn't anything to worry about, but it is there.

During this time, a new friend of mine had suggested a road trip to Glastonbury and I thought why not?

It was a misty day on the drive down and then the sun came out as we arrived – a beautiful metaphor in itself. We mooched around the shops and visited the Goddess Temple. We pulled oracle cards from the various decks that were available and spent time writing in our journals.

My friend said she was going to have a reading done, she had had them before and was drawn to book one. I, on the other hand, was a newbie when it came to psychic readings.

We had to choose between a man or a woman. The woman was a clairvoyant. I didn't even know what that meant at the time, but her face seemed friendly, so I went for it.

As soon as I sat down, she told me my Nan was there for me. I burst out crying. I was not expecting this at all. My Nan had recently passed away, and it was very close to her birthday, I was shocked that she could communicate with me through this lady. It was so special. She described her perfectly and I really felt her love and presence.

She also pulled some cards for me. One of which, I still remember. It was a picture of Earth and another planet next to it with lots of interesting drawings on it. The card was called 'Merlin's World' and she described it as if I had been living behind a big curtain and now it was being pulled back for me to see the truth. She said, your eyes have now been opened to a whole other world for you to explore. The spiritual world. The more you look, the more you will find.

Oh, how right she was.

My friend and I went for a cuppa and debrief after our readings and I knew in that moment that my life had been changed forever, my mind had been blown open. This was the green light I needed to begin the journey of embracing a more authentic life.

This is when I started to build my faith. I threw myself into learning and experiencing as much as I could. I attended many workshops and spiritual fayres; it was all so new to me, but it felt so right. Gong baths, Goddess temples, dream workshops, conscious festivals, Tarot groups and readings, spiritual development circles, shamanic journeying – you name it, I was there. I also collected an array of beautiful oracle cards and started learning more about Astrology at this point (more on this later).

My Leap of Faith

During this time, I was so happy and excited about life. I really felt that I had started to feel like me.

No longer trying to blend in or be what I thought I 'should' be.

The more time I spent doing what I loved, the more distance it created between me and my then husband. He was a logically minded spreadsheet man, and I was a full-on spiritual convert by this point.

Our relationship had always had its challenges, but we had found a way to work through most of them and communicate better with each other. We had shared a lot of really great times together, and had created what looked like a happy life, on the surface of things. But deep down, we both knew something wasn't quite right, and it had never felt quite right.

At this point, I booked an Astrology reading, I was going through a big shift and the session helped me to understand myself better and our relationship. The Astrologer gave me permission to be me. It was the first time I had felt properly seen by someone and I knew it was time to start a new more authentic chapter of my life. Sadly, this meant letting go of my marriage to a truly wonderful man.

This was and still is heart-breaking at times. But no matter how hard it has been to go through; I knew it was the best thing to do.

Until that point, my natural optimism was working against me, I kept hoping things would get better, there must be a way to 'fix' it. There must be a therapy that can help us. I tried everything but often the things we tried pushed us further apart. We were so different and for a long time that's what we both needed, to learn from each other. But eventually once we had learnt what we could from one another, those differences were our downfall. I was investing so much of my energy trying so hard to make the relationship something it could never be, it was exhausting. I had to admit defeat and let it go.

This decision had a major domino effect on all areas of my life. Once I gave myself permission to follow what felt right for me, I couldn't stop. At the same time, I decided to close my hypnotherapy practice of 5 years, sell my share of the house and all my belongings, and to top it all off- I had to say goodbye to one of the greatest loves of my life, our beautiful cat, Muffin.

I packed the limited stuff I had left into a very impractical suitcase (still way too much!) and followed my intuition, which was guiding me to Bali. So, cliché I know, but she was calling and so I went.

Learning to Open

I arrived in Bali late August 2018; I was signed up to a 5-week Sacred Femininity Tao Tantra Teacher Training, which didn't start for a few days. Reality suddenly caught up with me.

I checked into the guesthouse and felt so alone. It had been such a long time since I had travelled by myself. I had no-one with me to share the excitement of this trip with. I felt so sad. The grief hit me here. I cried and cried then slept for 13 hours straight, almost missing breakfast!

I find that grief hits you like a wave, sometimes big, sometimes small, almost always unexpected. It takes many, many waves of grief to get to a sense of peace again and even then, a new wave can show up out of the blue. You think you are over something and there it is again and again. I've learnt to allow the waves to roll through me. As painful as it is. It is a reminder of how deeply we care and feel as human beings.

The sleep had helped me acclimatise to my new situation. I was still feeling very fragile but that was OK and to be expected. I just had to take it day by day. I was glad I had something to focus on though with the course on the horizon.

I walked around the streets of Ubud and arranged to meet up with some of my fellow course mates. This put me at ease. They were other brave women willing to face their wounds with me. A community of like-minded people, structure, routine and deep healing were exactly what I needed. It was intense – the schedule ran from 7am until 8pm at night. We were using and learning lots of powerful techniques.

Sometimes I needed more time to integrate the shifts that were happening than the schedule allowed for. I didn't know that this was what I needed at the time.

The final week of the course was in a more remote area in the mountains, I could breathe here.

I started to respond to my own needs. To skip a class if it didn't feel right for me. To have a dance on the balcony by myself instead, or journal or sleep some more. It felt empowering to do this.

I was opening to receive the perfect guidance from my own body. This was the start of me finding my flow.

By the end of the course, I was very ready to fly the nest. The rest of the gang were heading back to Ubud for a closing ceremony, but I knew it wasn't for me. I set off further into the mountains in a taxi by myself. I had booked a hostel near some hiking trails and was ready to start my solo adventure.

This was tougher than I thought it would be. I really missed my community. I missed my friends and family. Suddenly, I was alone again. I'd created time and space I needed for the feelings that wanted to pass through me, without the distraction of others around me. But I wasn't willing to go there just yet. I found other ways to distract myself – namely obsessively watching tarot videos on YouTube to give myself false hope about my non-existent love life! This is actually how I taught myself tarot, so always trust that whatever you are doing even if it seems like 'a waste of time' is probably a very useful part of your journey. It's OK to soothe yourself with whatever works when you are going through a rough patch.

I spent a total of 2 months in Bali, moving from place to place as I felt guided to.

Sometimes I would be on an Island and not want to leave, extending my stay night by night. Other times, I was craving shops and city life and a bit of fun, including a trip to Asia's biggest Water Park on my own. I did whatever I felt like doing.

This is a beauty of travelling by yourself, you really can indulge every craving, however big or small. I went to a large cinema complex one day and opted for the VIP seat armed with bags of chocolate. It felt amazing to just give myself exactly what I needed, when I needed it. I was mothering myself.

A Mini Leap of Faith

My visa was coming to an end and I had pre-booked a flight to Malaysia before leaving England. I could not get excited about this. I had travelled a lot of Malaysia in a previous solo trip, and although I really enjoyed it, it wasn't calling me back. I stayed open to receiving an alternative idea.

I had heard a lot of my fellow travellers talking about how amazing Vietnam was, I hadn't been. I started to get excited by this idea and quickly looked up flights. It turned out that you had to change flights in Malaysia anyway to get to Vietnam. It only meant booking an onward flight. Result!

I made the decision to change my plan in less than 10 minutes then quickly applied for a visa, which took exactly the amount of time I had left – 3 days! Phew. Talk about cutting it fine.

This was a very good move.

Opening and Time to Rest

After a bit of travelling in the North, I ended up in Hoi An. Now this was my kind of place. While I was there, I was working at a beautiful yoga studio for a couple of weeks – this opportunity was another gift from the universe. I really needed to have a room of my own and some time to rest after a lot of moving around. I found the perfect place and was warmly welcomed. I was also lucky to have connected with 2 wonderful friends when out exploring by bike. They were my angels sent to help me through another challenging time.

Another Leap (Letting Go)

I was having a strained conversation with my then long-term best friend back home. I had felt the friendship was coming to an end for a little while, but until that point, I didn't have the strength to face it. The girls I had met really helped me through the experience, they were amazingly supportive.

People at home didn't agree with my decision to walk away from the friendship. They had seen or heard about the good things about our friendship, and of course there were plenty of lovely times otherwise we wouldn't have stayed friends for so long. I am grateful for the good and the bad. It's what my soul needed at the time. But what my soul needs at any given time changes, as I change. Big shifts within you, often accompany big shifts in the people you resonate with or not.

The lack of support for this decision from people at home made it even harder to go through. I had to cry about this too! It was a really shitty time but ultimately, I knew I was doing the right thing for me. I have never regretted this decision, but it was made more difficult by other people trying to sway me otherwise. This is part of the flow journey, sticking to what feels best for you no matter what people around you think or feel. I had equal amounts of challenge and support throughout all my big decisions in life.

Nowadays, I make big decisions and then tell my friends and family afterwards. I don't involve them in the decision-making process unless I need or want their help. I have learnt that some things are for me to figure out and to do, without the support of others. You know if what you are doing is not going to go down well with the people around you, when that is the case, don't tell them until you absolutely have to. You need to protect yourself and they will eventually understand why you did it that way. I've learnt that through oversharing my plans too many times and having my bubble of hope burst because of it. Now, I respect my own privacy.

Shortly after the 'break up' of my friendship my skin erupted with acne like never before. My body was clearing out all the anger I had felt towards the women in my life who had let me down. Some of this was ancestral stuff, past life and present life. It's amazing the physical reactions you can have to emotional situations.

Another Sudden Change (Leap)

Before leaving the UK, I had envisioned being away for a year, but something told me not to book the round the world ticket, and to only buy 3 months of travel insurance. I trusted this instinct even though I couldn't make sense of it at the time.

I was then surprised to find myself home for Christmas. It just suddenly made total sense to go home. I didn't know why, but I could not get excited about travelling anywhere else but home. It just felt right. I changed my flights on a whim one morning and surprised my family.

It was so lovely to see them, it had been a difficult time for us before I left. I pushed them away so that I could cope with what I needed to do. They thought I had lost the plot, and I felt like I had finally found the plot. I didn't have the energy to explain it at the time. I was trying to process it all myself. It was all too much; I went into survival mode and just did what I had to do.

Christmas was really special. I appreciated all the home comforts and being around my family. But then January arrived, and reality had caught up with me again.

Waiting

January 2019 was one of the toughest months of my life. Being back in Bristol was a constant reminder of what I no longer had.

I was back living at my parents' at 33 years old. I was very lucky to have this option, but it was far from ideal having previously been an independent homeowner. And, to top it all off, I had no winter clothes, I had given everything away. This was my rock bottom.

I entertained the idea of flying off somewhere else, but I knew it wasn't what I really needed. I had to stop running from myself and just feel and process all the pain and loss. I cried a river. I needed to. I had been holding back a tsunami for too long and finally I was ready to let it all out. This was exhausting. I was grateful to have a lovely family home to be in, with my supportive parents looking after me. I needed them even though I resisted it.

I didn't know where to begin with trying to put my life back together again. I was too broken to work. I needed to work on myself to figure out who I was now and what I wanted.

I started to do daily yoga and was focusing on building some structure and routine to my day. I signed up to an online astrology course, and this was just what I needed, a goal to focus on. I threw myself into the world of Astrology and discovered many of the answers I had been seeking.

Another Leap

Come April I was getting the nudge to go to Cornwall. I didn't know why but I was getting called – despite some resistance on my part.

I didn't want to leave my comfort zone, which to be honest had become uncomfortable. I had imposed on my parents for long enough, it was time to head off into the unknown again. I signed up to a house-sitting website, prompted by a big argument with my parents (a Tower moment!), and I took the first date available in Cornwall.

I was responsible for 4 cats, a dog and a pony! It was 2.5 weeks long and despite my nerves before going, I felt immediate relief when I arrived. I needed my own space and independence again. To be more connected with nature and myself. I had the most amazing summer enjoying coastal walks, sea swimming and taking good care of myself.

I connected with a spiritual development group, which was a wonderful lifeline for me. I also had a couple of friends who had already relocated to Cornwall, who were great at putting me up in-between my house sits.

It was all flowing along nicely until I tried to force my will on to the situation.

I'd met a guy at this point who was to teach me some very important yet brutal lessons about myself. I was drowning and I wanted someone to be my lifeboat. But I still hadn't really figured out what I really wanted or needed.

I started to dig my heels in. To cling to Cornwall. I didn't want to go with the flow anymore. I wanted to grab a rock and hold on tight.

But the universe had a better plan for me and made it very obvious that my time in Cornwall had come to an end. The housesits had dried-up, and even though I could stay at my friend's place while she was away, it suddenly didn't feel right anymore. I was no longer excited by Cornwall.

The intense but short-lived romance I had got swept up in came to an abrupt end. This was horrendous. I cried until 4am in the morning on the night it happened. Luckily, I had recently read 'The Universe has Your Back' and in my desperation, I asked the question – why is this happening FOR me? I repeated it many times over in my head and then I became peaceful enough to get some sleep. Even though I still couldn't see why, I had to trust it was all happening for my highest good. It felt like being punched in a bruise. I was NOT happy with the universe at all.

Why couldn't I just be happy now and start a new life? Hadn't I been through enough? Give me a fucking break!

What I didn't realise at the time was that I was far from ready for a new relationship. I needed to work on the one I had with myself first, and that was going to take a lot of time and some radical honesty.

Opening Again

At this point I was guided to read 'Calling in the One' – I had tried shunning this book for a while, but it kept coming back around like a bloody boomerang. Eventually, I surrendered and bought the book.

What a book. It was of course exactly what I needed to do the healing that I now recognised I so desperately needed. It was a 7-week course that I ploughed through in a couple of weeks. I saw it as my full-time job. I was lucky to have the time and space to dedicate to this and so I got to work.

For me, the book had little to do with meeting someone new. It was about learning to love and accept myself so much that I no longer needed to fill the void inside with approval or love from someone else anymore. It helped me to make sense of a lot of stuff from my past and make peace with it.

Another Leap

Christmas was fast approaching, and I had itchy feet again. This time Brighton was calling me. Totally random, I know! A surprise to me too but it popped into my head, and it felt good, so I went with it.

I found a 5-week short term let to rent, which meant I'd be home in time for Christmas.

On the drive down I felt so joyful, I could literally feel the flow. Like being swept along in a fun, fast current. It just felt right. I still had no idea why I was in Brighton, but I wanted to experience all it could offer. I worked my way through most of the local yoga studios and quickly discovered Kundalini yoga. This was an incredible find.

Until then I had been doing very gentle Hatha yoga via YouTube. This was upping the ante somewhat, and the spiritual aspect of the practice. There's a lot of chanting, breathwork and meditative repetitive actions. It was challenging but it stirred up my inner fire, which had been dampened for some time. I felt alive and energised after each class.

Opening to Meeting New People

One evening, I was feeling a bit lonely and happened to check online to see what was going on.

There was a Moon Circle being held that night and there was one ticket left- synchronicity at its best.

It was just what I needed, exactly when I needed it.

I also connected with a guy through a dating app who showed me just how far I had come from my last relationship. He was the perfect flirty friend for my time in Brighton, but not what I wanted or needed in a long-term relationship. I recognised this early and acted upon it, progress! Or so I thought. He just taught me different lessons.

Navigating something fleeting wasn't quite as easy as it sounds, I fluffed it up a lot. But when you take a new version of yourself out for a spin you may stall a couple of times before you figure out how to drive. And there is always more to learn. ALWAYS. Which means there are many more mistakes to be made and forgiven.

While in Brighton I read another amazing book about intuition that a friend from my tantra course had written. It was called 'Trust Your Magical Self', see recommended reading later. I devoured it in a few days and practised all of the exercises. It was the book I had always wanted to read. I was honing my skills and boosting my faith.

Opening More and Waiting

This is how I spent most of my time in Brighton, learning, nourishing myself, more letting go and healing. I was still shedding so much emotionally. I couldn't believe I had more stuff to cry about, it just kept coming. But I was grateful to have a private space just for me to do this, overlooking autumn trees.

I did also experience a lot of anger about it being someone else's space, full of their belongings and not my own. I allowed myself to feel the anger and frustration around this. I danced a lot to let the feelings move.

Deep down, I really wanted to have my own home again, but being self-employed and out of work meant this was not possible at the time. Or so I thought. I was limiting myself by only seeing one option. I wanted what I had already had – a home of my own, that was mine. At the time I wasn't prepared to entertain the idea of renting a flat long term. It wasn't the 'done' thing in my family. If I couldn't buy, I wasn't interested.

Leaving Brighton, felt much like leaving Cornwall, it was yet another loss to process. Some people or places stay for a while, some come and go with a flash. It doesn't mean they don't leave a lasting impact.

I did try and force my free will onto the Brighton situation too, by the way. That old habit of clinging to the known. I looked at options for moving there more permanently but it just wasn't flowing at all. I had to let it go with love and gratitude for the fun times I had had there. But I was upset about all the things I was leaving behind and this took a while to work through my system, like every loss. I headed back to Bristol for Christmas, listening to Frank Sinatra love songs.

And then there was January again. A whole year had passed and from the outside it looked like I hadn't achieved much at all, still single, jobless and living with my parents. Great! But from the inside I knew I had made significant progress.

I couldn't figure out my next move while under my parents' roof. Being there was no longer right for me or them, but I didn't want to make decisions out of desperation. I needed to hear my soul's voice, not my fearful mind or my parents' opinions.

A Little Leap

I booked a little eco cabin in West Wales at the end of January for 10 days to carve out some time and space to receive my next step. It was here that I wrote my first book. It flew out of me much to my surprise. A few chapters a day, and within a week I was done. It was very therapeutic.

Re-visiting my story enabled me to acknowledge just how much I had been through. It helped me to make sense of it all. I was proud of myself and could see how far I had come in a relatively short period of time. I was now totally comfortable in my own company and did not need to run from myself anymore. But what next?

By day 7, the lightbulb moment had struck. I pulled the tarot card 'the tower' that day. The epiphany was that it was time to put down roots, to commit to something again. To give myself what I wished others would give me. I needed my own space. My own home, even if I didn't own it!

The idea of Portishead, near Bristol, popped into my head. It had been in the background of my mind for a while, but I wasn't ready to entertain it before then. But suddenly it made total sense.

I had to experience all the moving around and living in other people's spaces before I could discover what I really needed and wanted.

I looked online for flats and I knew immediately that I had found the one. I booked to view it shortly after returning to Bristol and moved in within 3 weeks. It flowed! And funnily enough, the woman who was leaving the flat was selling all her furniture (handy for me) and heading off to Bali!

More Bloody Waiting!

Soon after moving in, Covid-19 happened, and I was locked down in my own lovely flat. This was another gift from the universe. Protected and precious time to really settle in, and to figure out my next step.

To slow down.

To give my roots time and space to grow strong and stable before attempting to grow again. To adapt to a new 'normal' life. Part of me felt like I was on hold again. Not quite sure what direction to take my business in. Having lots of passion and enthusiasm but nowhere to channel all of that energy. This was difficult. Many a meltdown, tantrum and harsh words with the universe were had. The waiting game again.

Looking back as I write this, I can see that I needed this time to build my connection to myself and my intuition, to get into good health and to learn what my writing style was. But at the time I was nothing but frustrated, confused and impatient a lot of the time.

But I just took each day as it came and did whatever I felt called to do. Exploring my new area on foot, focusing on my diet and health (my body had been screaming at me for a while). I connected with local spiritual people and set up a Monthly Moon Circle.

I had shelved the book I had written back in January, knowing it wasn't the time to do anything with it. But come April I was being nudged to revisit it. I read it for the first time since writing it and I was proud of it. It was good. It was time for action again.

LEAP

I contacted a publisher who worked with spiritual books and arranged a call to discuss the process.

Although he loved the raw honesty, he encouraged me to up the ante and to develop an actual philosophy to tie it all together. To take it to the next level. To start a movement. This excited me! I had learnt so much more I wanted to share.

OPEN

At first, I was overwhelmed at the thought of re-working the entire book. I let the idea sink in for a few days before acting. I needed to have a clear vision. I disconnected from social media and retreated. I read a lot, journalled, took long baths and walked in nature. I asked for guidance and listened to my inner voice and stayed very observant to the signs around me. Within a couple of days, I had received The Flow Philosophy. As I let it percolate my senses, I felt more and more eager to start writing again.

I began a new book with the idea of integrating some of the old into it. This didn't work. It quickly became apparent that the old book was for a very different audience and written by a very different person. I had moved on. I had discovered even more than before. The first book no longer felt like the message I wanted to deliver. I had something new brewing in me.

The sneaky Universe had tricked me into writing a whole new book and was asking me to let go of my previous one. For now, at least. Thank God I didn't know this in advance. I would have been far too overwhelmed to ever start writing if I had.

I had another leap of faith to make. Jump into the new book and let my old story go.

One year later

As I sit and re-read my story, it's changed. I've changed. My emotions around it have changed over time but I do still have emotions about it. I am feeling teary and sad that I ever had to go through so much hurt, pain and loss. I feel sorry for myself back then for having to face all of that mostly by myself.

I woke up feeling blocked and a bit off this morning, I was struggling to make decisions and feeling annoyed by small things. That, for me, is usually a sign that something wants to be felt. So here I am having a cry about it. Without judgement.

The waves of grief are much smaller now, but I still experience them. When it was all happening, I was good at putting a brave face on it, for others and sadly for myself too. My emotions were so deep, I couldn't even get to them. But now I am very much in touch with my emotions, I let them flow when they need to and I'm learning to like how emotional I am.

The changes in my life haven't stopped, I have been through many, many more cycles of Flow. I have lost more friendships, more homes, more job roles. It never ends. But I know and trust that with every cycle I fumble my way through, I am moving towards what is right for me and away from what is wrong.

What is easy to lose sight of is that I have gained as much as I have let go of. New and better friendships, new and better homes, and new opportunities to create and express myself through the connections I made on my travels.

Another lovely side effect is that I am closer to my family than ever before and I have realised how important family are to me.

PART 3

Let's Get Connected

So, How Do I Connect?

In order to live a '**go with the flow**' life you not only need a good understanding of the philosophy detailed in part 1 of this book, but you also need to spend time developing some necessary skills and tools to assist you along the way. That's what we will now explore.

Your best friend along this journey will be YOUR intuition, to start with you may need to lean on trusted intuitive people in your life but always be cautious with accepting any advice from friends or family. They have a particular agenda in mind for you which may not have the purest of intentions. They will want you to fit into the mould that they are used to seeing you in.

If you need outside assistance during your flow journey connect with someone who is neutral and feels right for you. But even then, do not accept their advice without checking in with how it feels to you. If anything they say jars with you, it may be an opportunity to override someone else's intuition with your own. This is part of the process of learning to trust yourself above and beyond anything or anyone else remember.

When I first started out, I would blindly follow tarot readers' advice, thinking they must have my answers, but they didn't. They had some very useful points to make but not all of it was for me to follow. I learnt the hard way that some of it was that old lesson rearing its ugly head again to TRUST MYSELF.

The universe will throw in curveballs every now and again. I'm not sharing this to scare you, I just want to make you aware of something that nobody told me!

You are the only expert on you.

Please question anyone who ever tells you, or makes you feel, otherwise!

Remember, these things take time to get the hang of but are well worth investing your energy in to.

I've got you. Imagine this book as a big warm embrace whenever you need it. Pick it up, hold it to your heart and feel the loving energy pouring out of it.

Trust and Develop Your Intuition

Being intuitive isn't about always getting it 'right'.

Sometimes you do and that's nice. But it's actually mostly a steep learning curve of constantly fluffing your way through life to learn from the many mishaps along the way.

I am recovering from an intuition complex. Assuming everyone else had my answers. I was tossed around like a bloody ping-pong ball for the first 30 or so years of my life asking everyone and anyone for their advice and acting on it. I still do on occasion!

The more people I asked, the more stressed and confused I became. Their advice sent me down many a wrong path.

Or so I thought.

Now I can see they were actually the right paths for me to learn what I needed to learn.

TO TRUST MYSELF.

So really, there is no right or wrong with intuition. It's just a constant process of learning through experience.

So...What is Intuition?

Intuition is your soul guiding you towards your important life lessons. These will inevitably involve quite challenging situations, circumstances and people.

This is why a lot of people choose to ignore their intuition, because it will always take you out of your comfort zone. Your soul is here to grow, and your intuition is your soul's voice. No growth happens in your comfort zone.

But the soul also knows the right pace and time for change, therefore it will never ask you to do something you cannot cope with. It knows you better than you know yourself. It also has access to the full picture, while you can only see a tiny piece of it at a time. This is to stop you from getting ahead of yourself.

Intuition is like a muscle that needs exercising. The more you use it the stronger it gets. But even when it is strong, you can still have your weak days. And that's OK and part of the journey.

How Intuition is Received

Intuitive nudges come in many forms. They are subtle and can easily be missed if you are not paying attention.

The spirit world, and your body, have to be very creative about how to get your attention.

A spark of inspiration, a new idea, a pull to do something, an opportunity presenting itself, a book to read, a gentle walk in nature with metaphorical signs and symbols, a hug and a chat with a special tree, an enlightening conversation with a stranger or friend, a persistent song, a spirit animal trying to grab your attention, a tarot reading, a boxset, a film, a poster or billboard, over-hearing someone else's conversation...the list is endless.

An intuitive insight feels uplifting, exciting and freeing, it might make you smile yet be a little bit scary.

How Intuition Works

You will only ever receive one step at a time.

This is where people become stuck. They try to reason with it. Well, if I don't know the future outcome of taking that first step, and the full 5 year + plan, then I can't possibly make that change.

This is where faith is needed.

If you knew too much of the plan upfront it would, A, spoil the surprise and B, totally overwhelm you.

It's the soul's job to feed it to you in bite-sized pieces. The next piece is ready for you, only when you are ready for it. You cannot rush this process.

It will be a small, and seemingly insignificant, action that you are being asked to take and you think 'what's the point in that'? You do not know where 'that' is leading you. Just trust that absolutely everything you are guided to do, no matter how big or small it may be, is super important to your life path.

Take each day as it comes. If the only thing you ever do is live in alignment with your intuition each day. You will always be on the right path, to your destination.

The destination is unknown. And always will be. You just take the directions as they come and be delighted by the journey along the way.

Real life example:

A while back I was guided to stop offering tarot readings – this confused me. I REALLY enjoyed giving tarot readings and I was good at it. Why stop? I did stop because it felt like the right thing to do and then my Astrology Readings took off. Then I was being guided to stop Astrology Readings just as they were taking off. I was again a bit perplexed by this and still am to be honest.

But my gut is telling me and has been telling me for a while now that working 1-1 isn't for me anymore. That actually I want to share my knowledge with a much wider audience. I don't know how or when I will be doing this, but I know I will. Or at least, I am hoping that will be the case, for now. Maybe this book will lead to opportunities? Maybe I'll have a new idea? Or maybe there is something even better than what I can imagine myself doing waiting for me?

I often find that you are asked to let go of things before you feel they are really done and way before you know what is coming next. It's worrying, like having the rug pulled from beneath your feet. Sit down for a bit before standing back up and just see what happens. It will all be revealed in time.

Important Stuff to Know about Intuition:

- Intuition is actually very subtle most of the time.

- It's metaphorical, not logical.

- You need to be quiet, calm and open to receive it.

- The messages vary in intensity depending on how necessary or important the message is for you to receive at that moment in time.

- Receiving clear guidance depends on your general mood, diet, sleep, energy levels etc.

- If the answer isn't clear either way, it is not the time for you to have an answer.

- No answer is an answer. Wait.

- If the thought or reality of something makes you feel stressed or anxious it's your intuition telling you, it's not for you!

- Sometimes you can be too emotional to see the wood for the trees. If you cannot find a way to be calm enough to connect it is probably time to book a healing session or psychic tarot reading. I do this too! Some things we just can't figure out for ourselves and that's OK.

Yes/No Exercise:

Call to mind a time where you made a decision that was 100% yes for you. Trust the first thing that comes to you.

Now, close your eyes and re-live that decision making experience. Notice how your body feels when it is a big fat yes. However odd or subtle the sensation is. Take note. Tune into your other senses too. Can you hear anything? Perhaps a song or a sound? Can you see anything in your mind's eye? A symbol? You may even have a taste in your mouth or a smell under your nose.

Make note of everything you noticed and were given, no matter how small.

Now do the same but for a decision you made that was 100% no.

Notice the difference.

Thank your body for communicating with you in this way. Ask it to use the same or similar signals for you to know and trust in the future.

Recommended Books:

Trust Your Magical Self: How to be Super Psychic, Extra Intuitive, and Love Your Sensitive Soul – Courtney Alex Aldor.

The Intuitive Way – Penney Pierce.

Be Curious and Creative

Creativity is an amazing tool to access and activate your intuition. When I started to allow myself to create in a playful way my intuition became supercharged.

Intuition speaks through our right brain – the creative part of us. Whereas logical thinking is all left-brain stuff. We want to activate the right brain as much as possible to light up our intuition like a Christmas tree.

This doesn't have to take a lot of time or require a lot of stationery buying. But I say go for it, if you want to!

Pretty much everything we do in our day to day lives can be seen as creativity in practice. For example, the way we dress, style our hair, decorate our homes, cook, shop, walk, work, move our bodies.

Don't panic, I was once filled with fear and dread if I was asked to draw, paint or make anything but now, having done it a few times I jump at the opportunity and really enjoy it.

I feel we might all have a similar fear around our own unique way of creating and the only way to overcome it is to face it, and all the emotions that come with it. I cried a lot through my first art class as an adult. I didn't even know why?! But it seemed very therapeutic.

Stuff to Know about Creativity:

- We are all creative beings by nature.

- Creativity is a fluid process, it's not linear and logical. It's magical.

- It's not about the final outcome.

- It's about the freedom of letting yourself go and feeling your way through the creative process one step at a time.

Creativity is play time for adults.

The possibilities are endless.

As a child you didn't think, "I can't draw, paint, write, etc because I'm not a trained artist, writer etc."

You just went for it. You didn't care about the outcome.

Until you learned to care about the outcome.

This is what needs undoing. The good news is – anything you have learned, you can unlearn. It just takes practice.

Create like no-one is watching. Create like no-one will ever watch. Experiment. Go crazy! If this sounds impossible right now then this is where your focus needs to be. Your creativity needs your attention immediately.

This can be as simple as committing to doing a daily doodle. Be as silly or simple with it as you like. A stick man or woman will do. See it as a starting point and then each day challenge yourself to do a little more or try something different. Use a different colour or type of pen. Change the size of the paper. Try creating with or without music on. See what happens.

You don't have to show anyone or frame it. You just have to allow your creativity some space to do its thing. You may be pleasantly surprised. You may cry. You may be super self-critical. That's all OK, keep creating anyway. Let your inner child out to run wild and free.

There are endless ways to be creative and every creative outlet is an opportunity to connect with and hone your intuition. Here are a few suggestions, to inspire you:

Creative Food Shopping

It starts in the supermarket. I never take a list.

As I walk into the shop, I ask my body to lead me to the perfect food for my nutritional needs at that point in time. I get magnetically drawn to different aisles and sections and certain foods appear more vibrant and appealing to me. I know that they are the ones that my body wants. Some aisles are an obvious no. Some I enjoy lingering in for a while finding what my body needs. This experience fascinates me. I get out of the way and let myself be led. It's fun, try it.

Be aware that your left brain (logic) will try and get involved, putting 2 and 2 together and making 10. You pick up one ingredient and you instantly begin the game of association. Oh, the last time I bought that, I made that.

That is the opposite of flow and creativity. You are trying to make logical sense of something that just won't. Allow yourself to be surprised. That ingredient could be used in any number of ways, not just the ways you are familiar with.

Just notice it when it happens and try your best to follow your guidance, even when it confuses you. This is hard, but the more you go with it, the more you surrender to what is best for you instead of trying to control the outcome of everything.

I try to only buy the ingredients I have been guided to, even if I can't make that particular dish without another particular ingredient. I trust there is a new recipe on its way, or within me to discover. Or if I don't buy the ingredient that my intuition told me to buy because I just couldn't make sense of it at the time, I am usually kicking myself later when I receive the perfect idea for how to use it! I'm not perfect, I'm still learning too. Fluffing my way through life, one mistake at a time.

Creative Cooking

Similarly, when cooking I ask my body what ingredients it needs, I start with the first step – maybe chop an onion, then I might be drawn to some spices or another vegetable. When creating mindfully you can never miss the next step, it is always revealed. Just give it time and space to do so.

Working with your spiritual guidance is like having your own in-built recipe book – sometimes you might need to do a quick Google search for inspiration but often if you follow what feels right it's better than any recipe. And all recipes come from someone's imagination anyway. Why not yours?!

As with all things intuition related, the calmer you are, the easier this is to do. If I start cooking when I'm already super hungry and tired. Game over. I miss a lot of the subtle signals my body is sending, and I'll be in a rush to whip something up. If I allow enough time and energy for the creative process,

I really enjoy it and I am often amazed by the results. Even when I don't 'think' it will work out well.

But sometimes it doesn't work out. Even if I am following my intuition. And that's OK, if a little disappointing! Each time it goes a little wrong, is a lesson in how to do better or make it differently next time. I have to just accept that I can't have perfectly balanced meals every single time because there is always more to discover about cooking and flavour combinations. And what my body likes or doesn't like at any given time. If you are trying something new it is likely that you will need to fuck up a few times before you figure it out. Sometimes it's delicious, and sometimes it's a bloody disaster!

Creative Walking

Allow yourself to be taken for a walk. Don't take yourself for a walk. Let go and be guided. Follow your nose. It knows!

Ask your body and guides to give you clear signals of which way to go. Clear signals can often be quite subtle in reality. That's why you have to be paying attention and get to know your own body very well.

Imagine going left and then imagine going right. Notice the changes that happen in your body. Which feels better? What is the difference? Give your body time to respond, it's not as fast as your mind.

Breathe and flow with the path that just feels right or even slightly better.

Even if it's a path you haven't walked before, try it. Sometimes you might meet a dead end. OK, turn around. Valuable lesson.

Sometimes you head down a path for a little bit and start to realise it's not for you, that's OK. Backtrack and go the other way. You don't know if something is right for you until you try it remember.

Intuition is not about always getting it right, it's a constant process of learning through experience.

Notice the second guessing which may come up — "Oh I must be going there." Maybe you are, maybe you aren't. Maybe you are going somewhere new which you haven't yet discovered. Focus only on the step that needs to be taken next, not future steps yet to be revealed.

I like to imagine that each new pathway or walk I find is opening a new pathway in my mind.

Remember to mindfully enjoy the journey and be open to the many surprises that can delight you along the way. For example, you might meet some lovely people and stop for a chat, or you might find some animals to connect with or a beautiful flower with an amazing scent, you might discover a new view or perspective of where you live.

Trust your instincts on when to go for a walk, not the weather forecast. We also know exactly what to wear to be comfortable during our walk. But our minds get busy trying to plan for every eventuality and we get confused. That's OK, just notice and try doing it differently next time. Every single experience, both big and small, is valuable when training yourself in the art of flow.

PART 4

Let's Get Practical

Flow Survival Kit

Flow life is hard, until you get the hang of it. And even then, it's still hard at times. But the good news is, you can make it easier while you are in training and beyond by connecting with the following tools.

You will need:

- Tarot

- Astrology

- Emotional Freedom Technique (EFT)

- Dowsing

- The Meltdown Method

Optional extras:

- Bach Flower Remedies (nature's very own pharmacy- I have the full set and would not be without them!)

- Alternative therapies – massage, reflexology, kinesiology

- Oracle Cards

- Readings with trusted psychics (the right reader will appear at the right time)

- Recommended reading books (see 'my faves')

Think of the toolkit as spiritual stabilisers. Comfort blankets. Supportive hugs. A lifeline. Or just a dose of hope, encouragement and relief whenever needed.

Please bear in mind that you don't need to, and definitely won't be able to master them all over night, just choose the one that really speaks to you and spend time with it. Then as and when you feel ready, choose another one to start learning about. It's taken me YEARS and many painful hours, courses and fuck ups to have these tools at my fingertips when I need them.

When starting out with something new, you are a 'Page' in tarot terms – someone who is super eager but lacking in experience, let yourself be a beginner, don't try and force yourself to be 'perfect and masterful' without giving yourself the time and effort required to get there.

I know it is frustrating starting out with something new, we want to run before we can walk! It was like me and writing a book for the first time, it's taken soooooo many attempts to find my style and my voice, and it has been frustrating as Hell along the way, but I am getting there. You do make progress, but it needs to happen one step at a time. One misstep at a time too! You only learn when you 'mess up' so allow that to be part of the journey. Then before you know it – you're the King or Queen in the tarot deck. Experienced and accomplished and ready to learn something else or perhaps teach others how to do it.

Tarot

Tarot is one of my favourite tools for connecting with my spiritual guidance and intuition. It has added much needed depth and understanding to the many complex situations I have encountered.

For me, reading tarot is an intuitive process. No surprise there! You do not need to know and understand the traditional meanings to benefit from connecting with tarot cards, but it can be helpful to learn them. If not, you can just use your intuition to guide you.

How to Use Tarot

Step 1: Start by choosing a deck that really speaks to you.

Not the one that you think you 'should' buy because everyone starts with that one (e.g., Rider Waite). Of course, you can if that feels right, but if another deck is drawing you in and makes you feel excited and happy, that's the one to go for.

I prefer decks that have lots of detail in the artwork, that way there is more to work with. Some of my favourite beginner decks include 'The Everyday Witch Tarot', 'The Light Seers Tarot' and 'Animal Totem Tarot'. They come with books that explain each card. I have since moved on to using decks without any booklets so that I just interpret them for myself.

Step 2: Get to know your Tarot Deck

Personally, I like to keep things very simple. Here's what I do:

When I get a new deck, I unwrap them and remove any packaging, then I place the cards in one hand and use my other hand to knock on them 3 times to clear the energy of wherever they have been before reaching me.

Then I start to work my way through handling each card in the deck, one by one, spending time looking at the artwork on the card to become familiar with it, and to charge each one with my energy.

Ultimately you need to find what works best for you. Some people love to charge their divination tools under the light of the full moon or using crystals. Some like to store them in silk scarves or special boxes. There is no right or wrong way to do this, there is only your way.

Step 3: Get shuffling and ask a question

Personally, I don't use any complicated spreads or elaborate methods for shuffling and pulling the cards. I actually barely shuffle them.

I just take 3 deep breaths before shuffling the cards. I do this while asking a question either out loud or in my head. I usually keep the question very simple and non-specific like, "What do I need to know in this moment?" Or "Please can I have guidance or insight for the day ahead?"

I keep shuffling until something jumps or falls out of the deck and work with those cards. It's usually less than 3 cards, typically I work with 1 or 2. If nothing jumps out, I know I might not be using the right deck, or it might not be the right time to ask the question. Or I might be asking the wrong question. Over time you get to know these things.

Less is most definitely more when reading Tarot. The more time you spend with each card, the more it will reveal to you. Working with lots of cards creates confusion and dilutes the message.

Step 4: Read the Tarot Cards

To read the cards just say what you see and feel. Describe the card in as much detail as possible. I'd recommend either saying it out loud or writing it down in a journal to be able to refer back to.

Here are some questions to get you started:

How does the card make you feel?

What colours do you notice? What do they mean to you?

Can you describe what is happening in the card?

What type of energy does it give off? Happy, sad, confrontational etc?

What part of the image really stands out to you?

What feels less important?

How are the characters in the card feeling? What are they doing?

Which character or image represents you?

Is there a theme or story that plays out across the cards?

Does the card remind you of anything? A song? A person? A sound? A smell?

How does this information relate to what you are currently experiencing?

Trust whatever comes to mind and remember you have to be open to hearing some things you might not want to hear. That's the trick with reading tarot for yourself. You have to be super honest and not just say what you want to see. This takes time and practice. Stick with it.

When starting out I would highly recommend pulling a card daily. I usually pull a card after I've had a shower or have done some yoga, I feel cleansed and ready to start my day and it feels appropriate to do it then. But sometimes I just grab them whenever they call me and/ or I feel like it.

The ultimate goal of working with tarot is to provide you with guidance and direction, understanding and hope, for the here and now. Always focus on the present moment.

Contrary to popular belief tarot cards do not predict your future. Your future depends on what you do today.

Suggestion

- Buy a beautiful tarot deck which makes you smile and start connecting with them on a regular basis using the questions above.

Astrology

Who am I and why the hell am I here? I've asked these questions for as long as I can remember.

After much searching, I found my answers by exploring the world of Astrology.

You are not just your 'Star Sign' or 'Sun Sign'. You are influenced by a very complex blend of many different energies.

The moment you entered this life you were psychologically branded by the position of the planets at an exact point in time. They made their permanent mark on you, in a very unique way, determined by your time of birth, location and date. When you put this information into software which can draw your birth chart for you (I use astro.com), you will see a circular diagram with lots of lines, symbols and numbers on it. It looks complicated, because it is. As are you!

Having an Astrology reading was one of the most validating experiences of my life. It confirmed who I was and what I was about, what I am here to do and my unique approach to doing it. Stuff that I already knew on some deep level, but now I had permission to get on with it.

But we have free will.

At first, I had massive resistance to the things that my birth chart suggested would be helpful for me to do and embrace. I stubbornly continued to do it my preferred way for a long time before I finally surrendered. I was getting nowhere, and it was frustrating the Hell out of me.

Overtime, I slowly began to succumb to my fate and move towards the difficult things I had been avoiding. To 'go with the flow' of my birth chart. It took a lot of conscious effort on my part. It's not easy following the path that was chosen for you, there are many challenges, but the rewards outweigh them.

We are all so wonderfully different. But we often try to hide our differences to fit in. Or we take our natural talents and interests for granted as something everyone can do, or as not important. We need to celebrate all of our quirks and find the courage to share them openly.

Suggestions:

- Book a reading with an Astrologer – prepare to be amazed!

- Start to study and explore your own chart.

- If you do not know your birth time, you can try dowsing or work with a kinesiologist who may be able to help determine this for you.

Emotional Freedom Technique

We all need some form of healing or 'self-soothing' as I like to call it.

This is essential, not optional to living a flow life.

Your emotions will be triggered A LOT, especially at the beginning of the journey. Your fears and pain will come to the surface as and when you are ready to fully face it. The tool I have found most helpful for these moments is Emotional Freedom Technique (EFT).

EFT is a simple technique you can learn to do on yourself. I use it often. It involves gently tapping on specific meridian points (the main energy lines that run through your body) to release whatever symptom you are experiencing.

It provides instant relief and can be used on emotions and/or physical symptoms. The beauty of this technique is that you do not need to fully understand the symptoms you are experiencing to be able to let them go.

The feeling or physical ailment you are experiencing is just your body telling you what it needs or wants you to release. Emotions don't need to be understood logically, they just need to be moved through the body. Your body holds onto all the trauma and upset you have experienced throughout your life. That's why it's super important to release it not only mentally but physically too.

During an EFT session you will notice yawning, sighs, stomach gurgles, shivers, burps even, as you begin to release the symptom from the body. This is very satisfying!

This is a simplified 'use at home' version of EFT, which I use, and it works wonders. You can of course work with a qualified EFT practitioner to do this too. Healing doesn't have to be expensive; it can be free and easy if you learn how to do it yourself.

Beginners Guide to EFT

Step 1: Check in with yourself

Start by acknowledging the problem you want to self soothe – is it an emotion, a situation or a physical niggle?

Begin with a body scan to notice any signals or signs your body is trying to show you. Just close your eyes and scan down from the top of your head and keep moving your attention down through your body while taking note of anything that is being flagged as a problem, e.g., tightness in right shoulder, or fluttering feeling in stomach, stabbing pain in belly button. Do not discount anything, even the smallest of symptoms are significant. It can be absolutely anything and is often very random.

If you feel nothing or you don't know how you are feeling e.g., you feel numb to your feelings or your body, you can tap on that too. It all works no matter how bizarre it may seem.

You will get better at noticing the small things the more you tune in and work with your body in this way.

Step 2: Identify the Main Problem

Now choose just one of the symptoms or emotions you have identified to work on first. Go with the one that feels the most obvious or strongest in that moment.

Step 3: Set the Scene for Healing

Start by locating meridian point 1 (detailed below) and then gently and continuously begin to tap on it using several fingertips simultaneously of the opposite hand. Choose whichever hand you prefer to work with.

Meridian Point 1: Karate chop point on the side of your hand, the soft squishy part on the outer side of your palm (used for step 3 only)

While you tap on meridian point 1, say the following statement out loud or in your head:

"Even though (insert your main problem here...for example...I feel numb, or my belly button hurts, or I am really sad today and can't be bothered to do anything). I love and accept myself completely."

Repeat the above statement 3 times, while tapping on meridian point 1, before moving on to the next step.

Step 4: Start the Healing

Now begin to move around the other meridian points (listed below) while focusing only on repeating your chosen problem over and over again. E.g., I feel numb, I feel numb, I feel numb.

You do not need to repeat the full statement from step 3, just focus on the problem itself.

Below are the Meridian points you need to tap on – remember to use only the fingertips of one hand to do the tapping. A very light tap is all that is needed. When I first started doing EFT, I gave myself bruises!

Meridian Point 2: Top of your head (middle scalp area).

Meridian Point 3: Start of the eyebrow (the inside).

Meridian Point 4: Bone on outer side of the eye (you don't have to do both sides, just choose the one that feels easiest for you to work on).

Meridian Point 5: Bone directly under the eye.

Meridian Point 6: Top of the lip.

Meridian Point 7: Beneath your lower lip.

Meridian Point 8: Just under your collarbone.

Meridian Point 9: Your inner wrist.

Work your way through meridian points 2-9 at a pace that feels right for you. When you really hit the spot where it is held you may feel like crying, or a wave of heat, or a shiver – let it flow, this is a very powerful form of release.

Step 5: Stick with the same problem until something shifts

Repeat step 4 as many times as you feel you need to while keeping the focus on the same symptom.

You will know when something has shifted, as you will feel a whole lot lighter and relaxed.

When you start to feel better and like the symptom has eased or disappeared you can start the process again from step 3 with your next most prominent symptom.

Continue working through different symptoms as they arise. When you are done clearing one, another will be shown to you.

Keep in mind that there are many layers to any problem so keep going until you feel a session is complete. Take time to rest afterwards if you can, to fully let the healing settle into your system.

Even 5-10 minutes of this technique can be a total game changer.

Dowsing

My life changed when I discovered how to dowse. I cannot believe this is not more widely known about and used. It is so simple and super helpful.

Like Tarot, dowsing is a divination tool used to connect you with your spiritual guidance and intuition. Dowsing when using a pendulum enables you to ask questions and receive yes or no answers. This can be incredibly reassuring when you are wanting to make a decision about something and are seeking some confirmation that you are doing the right thing. It's like having a hotline to your higher self.

As with all divination techniques, there are lots of different ways to approach it. Here is the way I do it:

Step 1: Select a Dowser

I would recommend buying an actual pendulum to work with. They cost around £10-£15.

Pendulums are generally a pointed crystal on the end of a short chain. They are specifically designed for dowsing, and as such are well weighted and have a natural point at the end. This makes it easier to clearly identify the answer indicated, especially when there are multiple answers available.

But no worries if you don't have one, you can use a crystal on a necklace, a key on a piece of string or something similar. Get creative and make sure you love using it.

Step 2: Set up a Dowsing Chart

Start by drawing a simple dowsing chart on a piece of paper. This is a semi-circle with equally sized segments for each of the possible answers available to your question e.g., start with 3 equal segments with 'yes', 'no' or 'ask a different question'.

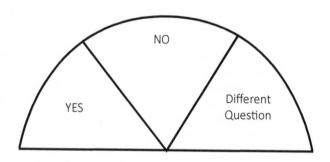

Step 3: Cleanse your Crystal and Set an Intention for it

If you have chosen a pendulum or a necklace with a crystal on it then it is important for you to cleanse it and set an intention for its use.

Simply place it in the palm of your left hand and blow on it 3 times, imagining that your breath is cleansing the crystal of any old stagnant energy.

Then lightly place your right palm over the top of the crystal while it is still in the palm of your left hand and set your intention for the crystal.

Start by calling in the presence of your faith of choice (angels, spirit guides, ancestors etc) and saying something like:

"Angels please be with me to help cleanse and set the intention for this crystal."

Then set your intention:

"I set the purpose of this crystal as the giver of clear and helpful guidance through dowsing."

I'd suggest doing this on a fortnightly basis, you could make it a ritual that you do at both the full and new moon each month.

Step 4: Start Asking Questions

Start by asking your question, either in your head or out loud and gently swing your pendulum of choice in a small circle at the centre point of the semi-circle. Then, wait for the pendulum to naturally swing into and settle on one of the sections with an answer.

Ta-da! So simple but oh so useful.

It is good practice to begin with the question: is it a good time for me to dowse?

It takes a little time to build up a strong connection with your dowser. Be patient and open to developing this. You can use simple questions that have a yes or no answer that you already know, like "Is my name …? Was I born in …?" To get a feel for it.

How to Ask Questions

Keep it specific, include a timeframe if possible and have a way for spirit to be able to guide you to the right question so that you get the guidance that you need.

For example, if you ask, Shall I finish painting the fence? The answer may well be yes, but your spirit guides might not want that to happen today, but you did not specify a timeframe. So, it would be better to ask: "Shall I finish painting the fence now? Or today?" It might then be 'no'. But if you ask the following day it might be 'yes'.

Adding an option of 'ask a different question' to your dowsing sheet will help you to prevent these simple misunderstandings.

I tend to ask, "Is it in my highest interest to....?" So that I know I am in alignment with what is best for me at any given time.

Suggestions for Use

Once you have mastered yes/no questions you can move on to more detailed scenarios:

- You could dowse to see which stage of flow you are in or which one is most difficult or easy for you. Just divide the semi-circle into 4 sections – Faith, Leap, Open and Wait.

- You can use it to figure out what your priority is on your to-do list. Write out all the things you need or want to do and then ask which is most important, or which one should you start with. Add an 'other' option in case there is something you are missing.

- You can use it in a healing session. I combine it with EFT to really get to the root of what I am feeling. You can ask what emotion you need to feel, or which physical symptom is your priority to work on.

- Or what foods your body likes/ dislikes – you can write 'harmful, beneficial or neutral' or 'eat frequently, sparingly, never' and then ask about different food groups e.g., dairy, grains, gluten.

The possibilities really are endless! There are lots of dowsing charts freely available online so take a look for inspiration.

I mostly use dowsing when I'm having a clear-out of my belongings – I write 'keep, giveaway, sell, other' and then work through my wardrobe or other items.

It really helps you to let go. If there is resistance to letting the item go then you may need to wait until it feels easy or do some journaling or healing around why it is difficult. Resistance means there is an emotional attachment that needs your attention or that you actually want to keep it, for now at least. And that's OK. Only let go when it feels right. But letting go always requires a leap of faith.

A Word of Warning

With all things, TRUST YOURSELF, not the dowser. It is just a helpful tool; it is not gospel. I have learnt some very difficult lessons by mindlessly following what the dowser told me to do despite my reservations and now if the answer ever jars with me then I know, I am right, and it is teaching me to trust myself above and beyond everything.

I realise this is confusing for a beginner to get their heads around, but I want to be real about this. Remember, the dowser is connecting you to your intuition and spiritual guidance. This will always lead you towards what you need to learn so whatever the answer is, it doesn't guarantee it will be plain sailing ahead.

Dowsing can be addictive – use it sparingly. I've over-used it at times and suddenly my dowser would mysteriously go missing! I even bought a new one and accidently dropped it on the floor and it smashed. Your guides will find a way to let you know if you are overdoing it!

Remember your body is the ultimate dowser. You don't need any of these tools, they are just fun short cuts for occasional use, practice and reassurance.

Troubleshooting

If the pendulum keeps spinning in a circle or wobbling you may need to ask a different question or word the question you asked in a slightly different way.

Make sure you are clear and calm when dowsing. Go for a walk, do some yoga or meditate if you are receiving confusing answers.

Focus your questions only on the present moment, or very near future and be specific.

Suggestions:

- Buy, make or find a pendulum you love.

- Start practising just for fun.

- Create your own dowsing charts.

The Meltdown Method

I use all of the above tools and techniques, but I have also discovered my own way to do 'emotions'.

I'm calling it the 'Meltdown Method'. It's simple but super effective.

Step 1: Acknowledge defeat

Stop trying to put a brave face on it.

When you feel like you are at tipping point, everything seems too much, lots of things are bothering you and you are quick to react with anger or upset then just STOP what you are doing and grab a pen and paper, or your laptop.

Step 2: Write that shit down

Sit down and go to town with writing a list.

Title the list: **THINGS THAT ARE FUCKING ME OFF**

Write EVERYTHING on the list, big, small, ridiculous and hilarious. Capture everything that is getting on your nerves, all the things you have probably been trying to ignore or pretend are ok for a while.

Acknowledge them ALL. They want to be seen and witnessed and to get out of your head and be felt!

Keep going until you have exhausted every single last thing. Be REALLY honest with yourself, don't hold back. Make sure no-one will ever see the list so you can be properly brutal with it. Write in capital letters if it helps express your anger or emotions.

Some of the things that have featured on my lists have made me laugh out loud because they seem so silly, but they are bothering me, nonetheless.

Step 3: Spot patterns

Once you have captured the list, stop to see if there is a recurring theme or pattern to your problems, are you people pleasing? Are you not following what you REALLY want to do? Are you suppressing your emotions? Trying to keep the peace? Going along with what other people want?

Step 4: Dig Deeper

Choose the one that is REALLY bothering you the most and write about it in detail.

This will help you to get to the emotion beneath it all. Keep writing until you hit a nerve, the tears will start flowing at this point. Cry like a baby if you need to. I do.

You don't have to sit and try to find solutions to the problems; this is not what this process is about. You'll often find that solutions magically appear once you have been properly honest with yourself and felt your emotions.

Blocked emotions, block solutions. Free the emotions to create movement and clarity.

Step 5: Let it go

When this process feels complete, you need to delete, destroy or burn the list in whatever way feels most fun and cleansing for you.

Step 6: Get it out of your system and your space

Next, shake it off with a dance or some other form of movement that you enjoy, or take a shower or bath to wash it all away. Open the windows or doors to clear the air in your space.

Step 7: Celebrate!

Give yourself a BIG pat on the back for doing this hard work! Now, reward yourself in some way e.g., hot bath, nice meal, film night, duvet day, whatever you LOVE to do, do it.

Repeat this method often!

Some Final Thoughts...

Going with the flow does not mean you get your way all of the time, in fact you rarely get your way. I'm sorry to disappoint, but it's true.

You signed up to learn some big lessons in this lifetime and so you get the way that teaches you the most about yourself and helps you to grow into an even better version of who you really are. Which is actually much better than having it your way.

But it's a really rough ride at times. It is, I'm not going to sugar coat it and try to sell you the 'dream life' that doesn't exist.

A dream life would be bloody boring if you ask me, without the challenges, where are the triumphs? The "Fuck yeah, I did it" moments, or the "Wow, I got through that" or "Go me for persevering despite all the setbacks." Yes, alright, I realise this is annoying to hear as we'd all love a shortcut to success, love and happiness but it's not going to happen.

My hope is that despite the difficulties you will inevitably encounter along the way, I have inspired you enough to do it anyway- to face the many challenges head-on, to not give up when the going gets tough, to keep the faith no matter what.

Always remember that REALLY going with the flow is paradoxically the most natural, yet challenging way to do life.

What I have come to realise through the process of writing this book, and much playful experimentation is that to really flow, we need to fall out of it often and then FEEL our way back into it.

To leave flow, is part of flow.

We need to allow ourselves the time, space and freedom to try out different options to know how it feels.

Because it is only through the felt experience of each option that we can truly know and choose the one that feels right for us. Like Goldilocks and her porridge.

But it is, as we are, ever-changing.

When we flow, we keep choosing again and again and again, refining and raising our standards each step of the way. What was right for you yesterday, may not be right for you today and that's OK. It can change in a heartbeat.

The old you must die so that the new you can be born. They cannot exist simultaneously. This will happen many, many times over.

Be brave.

Because to get what you REALLY want, you have to say no to what you DON'T want and trust that something better is on the horizon. It really is as simple, and as difficult as that.

Don't settle for less, make space for more.

My Faves

Embracing Flow Life

Change Me Prayers: The Hidden Power of Spiritual Surrender - Tosha Silver.

The Universe Has Your Back – Gabby Berstein.

Intuition Development

Trust Your Magical Self: How to be Super Psychic, Extra Intuitive, and Love Your Sensitive Soul – Courtney Alex Aldor.

The Intuitive Way – Penney Pierce.

Self-Soothing/ Healing

The Secret Language of Your Body – Inna Segal.

Calling in 'The One' – 7 weeks to Attract the Love of your Life – Katherine Woodward Thomas.

Acknowledgements

Thank you to my family for being the rock to my ever-flowing fire and water. I bloody love you all.

Thank you to all the friends and boyfriends I have ever had for teaching me how to value myself and to speak my truth...with kindness.

Thank you to my spirit guides, the angels, ascended masters, lost loved ones and whomever else I connect with, I feel your love and presence on a daily basis, and I am so grateful to now have such a strong connection with you.

Thank you to Lydia and Pia, the 2 angels I met while in Vietnam, I am so grateful for you both.

Thank you to my publisher, Sean, for believing in me right from the start, and for inspiring me to reach higher.

Thank you to Tina Huckle, Tanya Strike, Kim Lane and Jenny Hughes for boosting up my confidence and supporting me along the way with your delicious Earthiness!

Thank you to Gail Dey (Teawings Tarot) for being so brutally honest with me and for guiding me back onto my path whenever I am lost!

Thank you to Yoga with Adriene, I love your energy and your videos have got me through many a tough time.

Thank you to all the authors before me, whose books helped me along the way and still do!

And finally, a MASSIVE thank you to you...the reader! For choosing this book, for taking the time to read it, for stepping into my weird and wonderful world. I am so grateful for you and I really do hope it touches your heart and soul in both big and small ways.

BIG LEO LOVE,

Dani xx

Lightning Source UK Ltd.
Milton Keynes UK
UKHW011453141021
392146UK00004B/121